TRANSFORMATION
OF THE
NEGRO AMERICAN

TRANSFORMATION
OF THE
NEGRO AMERICAN

Leonard Broom and Norval D. Glenn

HARPER COLOPHON BOOKS
Harper & Row, Publishers
New York, Evanston, and London

Contents

Acknowledgments

This book was aided by several organizations. We thank the officers and the personnel of the Center for Advanced Study in the Behavioral Sciences, the Hogg Foundation of the University of Texas, the University of Illinois Research Board, and the University of Texas Research Institute.

For supportive interest and scholarly counsel we are grateful to Phyllis Barnett, Benjamin Bradshaw, Nathan Hare, Wayne H. Holtzman, Millard H. Ruud, John R. Stockton, Robert L. Sutherland, Ralph Tyler, and W. Gordon Whaley.

For service beyond the job description we thank Joydene Wheeler.

Gretchan Broom with her Fowlerpiece shot down flocks of infelicities and solecisms. In the current printing we hope our retriever has served her better.

L. B.
N. D. G.

Introduction

This book is written at a time of urgency in domestic affairs in the United States reminiscent of the Depression and of national cleavage unknown since the Ku Klux Klan marched in the 1920s. A heightened popular awareness has been fostered by sustained publicity characteristic of wartime. Tensions are focused upon a new element in the national life: the transformation of Negroes from a voiceless people largely dependent on white benefactors and vulnerable to white opponents to a people still vulnerable to whites but discovering new avenues of influence.

The end product of the transformation of the Negro American cannot be clearly foreseen. There are forces tending toward the creation of a Negro proletariat, even a black nationalist proletariat. There are forces tending toward a more even distribution of Negroes through the niches of opportunity and reward. There are forces representative of the national interest, and often mistakenly thought to be restricted to the North, that are devoted to accelerating and implementing the latter trends. There are forces, most conspicuous in the South but not restricted to the South, that persist in a delaying action that has been going on since Reconstruction, that prefer to postpone steps toward racial equality in the United States until the generation of their children or their grandchildren. Many of those who now resist change were made hostages to the future by parents who could not bring themselves to welcome Negroes as apprentices to equality in the American society.

Negro discontent was born of slavery. The expression of that discontent was born of hard-won progress. If there were no Negro college graduates and lawyers, no Negroes with substantial earning power, no Negroes with a sophisticated sense of obligation toward their fellows, there would be no sit-ins, no freedom marches, no Civil Rights Bill. Protest has become legitimate because Negroes learned to apply the egalitarian ethic to themselves. But all forms of protest have not become legitimate. The Negro middle classes had to learn how to mobilize their efforts, and in the course of their learning they released the energies of the rest of the Negro population. Now, undereducated and poor Negroes express long-harbored resentment, but only part of their discontent is directed at improving their condition.

Despite the uncertainty of the days just ahead and the risk that the news of tomorrow will prove the sociology of today to be in error, we have tried to identify the major trends and assess the chief impediments to change as well as the thrusts toward further change. In the first four chapters, we trace the emergence of the major themes in the adjustment of Negro Americans to subordination: compliant adaptation, self-improvement and gradualism, Negro nationalism, and increasing and increasingly overt pressure for integration. These several themes are expressed as shifts in emphasis rather than an evolution through clearly defined stages. In the next four chapters we take a hard look at the hard data about the condition of Negroes. We compare them with whites at several points in time and we evaluate the trends so far as the evidence allows. In the spheres of education, income, and occupation we try to show how much progress has been made, where the Negro stands, and what the remaining gaps are between Negro and white. We also show how the several aspects are interrelated and influence each other, and we estimate how the present condition of the Negro is likely to affect his ability to improve his future condition.

In writing this book we decided to address ourselves to the general reader and not merely to our colleagues with whom we could conspire to communicate through the short-cuts of professional vocabulary and statistical analysis. Instead, we have tried to use everyday English and simple arithmetic. We hope we have not sacrificed the power of sociological perspectives. We write as sociologists, but we have not followed all the lines of analysis and exposition that we would have pursued had we been writing solely for a professional audience.

Through the growth of protest activity and the civil rights debate and the cloture vote and the bill's passage and "the long hot summer" of 1964, we were constantly reminded that we were trying to understand phenomena of the greatest consequence. We resisted the impulse to be deflected by a particular event or to be carried along on a wave of popular interpretation. We have not resisted the sense of urgency and currency, because they are part of the phenomena we try to understand. But we do strive to see the urgent and the current in the context of the longer processes of the transformation of the Negro American and the evolution of the American society.

The University of Texas   LEONARD BROOM
Austin   NORVAL D. GLENN
August 1964

Preface to the Paperback Edition

This new printing is purged of a number of discrepancies but it is by no means a revised edition. In a few places the latest available statistics have been supplied. We have also added several new titles to the bibliography and a postscript, "A Perspective from 1967," beginning on page 191.

We take this opportunity to emphasize that our use of the term Negro American is a deliberate inversion of conventional usage. We mean to imply that the transformation involves a casting off of the Negro's uniquely subservient status and the assumption of some characteristics of immigrant minorities. "Negro American" suggests what we perceive as a trend but a trend far from complete.

In the early pages of this book we attempt a rapid historical review to remind the reader of the background of recent events and to identify the sources of some persisting and some obsolescent influences. We then turn to an analysis of emergent forces and try to make objective assessments of the direction and rate of change. If the consequences of action and public policy are to be responsibly evaluated, it is essential to establish base lines and trend lines. This we have tried to do.

Austin
April 1967

LEONARD BROOM
NORVAL D. GLENN

TRANSFORMATION
OF THE
NEGRO AMERICAN

1

Adjustment to Freedom

Emancipation and Reconstruction

When Lincoln issued the Emancipation Proclamation on January 1, 1863, more than a tenth of all Negroes in the United States—almost half a million—were already free. The free population had grown rapidly after the Revolution, by emancipation in the Northern states and manumission of individuals, many of whom were illegitimate children of their white masters. In the larger cities, some free Negroes were artisans, and in a few cities, such as Charleston, they had a virtual monopoly of the skilled trades (Frazier *b*, p. 70). In contrast to the slave population, most free urban Negroes were literate (Frazier *b*, p. 74). Overall, however, the condition of free Negroes was not good. In Northern cities, competition from white workers limited entry into better paid occupations, and Negroes were often the objects of violence. A few rural Negroes became substantial landowners and even slave owners, but most remained impoverished. In the South, free Negroes formed an intermediate social stratum, above slaves, but well below whites. In the North they had a more ambiguous status but were denied social, political, economic, and educational equality.

The slaves freed at the end of the Civil War were very different from those who had gained their freedom earlier. Although a few had been artisans and service workers as slaves, the vast majority had no skills except as agricultural laborers, and almost all were illiterate. Since they had never before directed their own lives, it is not surprising that when the social controls of slavery were suddenly removed, there was widespread chaos and disorganization among the freedmen.

The federal government did not ignore the problems of adjustment to freedom. In 1865 Congress created the Freedmen's Bureau, which was active through the early Reconstruction Period. The Bureau developed a widespread system of public education for Negroes, and such Negro universities as Howard, Fisk, and Atlanta were founded or substantially aided. Soon after its formation, the Bureau received nearly 800,000 acres of land and 5,000 pieces of town property that it leased to former slaves. However, President Andrew Johnson's proclamation of amnesty restored most of this property to its former owners, and the Negro tenants were dispossessed. The long-term effects of the Bureau's efforts were considerable, but the immediate social and economic problems of the freedmen were too great for its meager powers and resources.

The Thirteenth, Fourteenth, and Fifteenth amendments to the Constitution gave the Negro citizenship, the franchise, and equal protection under the law, and during Reconstruction federal troops stationed in the South enforced the new legal rights. Consequently, Negroes became politically powerful throughout the South and were a majority of registered voters in some states. Many were elected to state legislatures (although they never controlled any legislature), fourteen were elected to Congress, and two went to the Senate.

Not surprisingly, illiterate, unsophisticated Negro voters often did not use the franchise wisely, and they were vulnerable to manipulation. Negro officeholders were of greatly varying capability, but many, especially at the state and local levels, were incompetent. The former slaves were on the average inept and were duped by the unscrupulous. Some well-educated free Negroes,* however, were capable and interested in preserving order and economic stability. On the whole, Reconstruction governments were not models of efficiency, honesty, and responsible exercise of authority, although they probably were not the egregious examples of corruption and "savage rule" that many Southern editors portrayed them to be.

Reconstruction lasted for scarcely more than a decade, hardly long enough for impoverished and ignorant ex-slaves to make much headway in closing the cultural and economic gaps between themselves and whites. In spite of the legal rights granted to Negroes, they did not have really equal opportunities, and except for some free Negroes, they were ill-equipped to take advantage of the opportunities they had. Many forms of discrimination persisted or originated during Reconstruction, and Negroes became even more isolated than before. In the absence of the paternalistic and self-interested care of white masters, the health of many Negroes deteriorated. Hunger, intemperance, and adverse living conditions took their toll, and the Negro death rate rose above that of the late slavery period (Frazier *b*, p. 568). Freedom and equal rights under the law could not in so short a time bring about appreciable improvement in the condition of Negroes.

Subordination and Acquiescence

One can only speculate how rapidly Negroes would have advanced if they had been able to retain the franchise and equal legal rights. As it happened, their newly gained freedom was in large measure taken from them before they had a chance to adjust to it and take advantage of it. Starting with

---

* We distinguish "free Negroes," who had won their freedom before the Emancipation Proclamation, from the rest of the population who were emancipated.

the Compromise of 1877, whereby the Democrats agreed to the election of Rutherford B. Hayes, a Republican, to the Presidency, in return for withdrawal of the remaining federal troops in the South, Northern whites step by step withdrew their support for equal Negro rights, and white supremacy was restored in the South. The franchise was gradually withdrawn from the Negro, first by intimidation and then by such means as poll taxes, literacy tests, and white primaries. New forms of discrimination and segregation—for instance, in public transportation—were legislated into existence, often before they were widely practiced. By the turn of the century most forms of segregation known as "Jim Crow" were practiced (Woodward, chap. 2), although few of these types of segregation existed during Reconstruction or for a decade or two thereafter.

During the last three decades of the nineteenth century, the United States Supreme Court, responding to the temper of the times, made a series of decisions adverse to Negro rights—decisions that helped reconcile North and South at the expense of the Negro. For instance, in *Plessy v. Ferguson* (1896) the Court established the "separate but equal" doctrine, and two years later, in *Williams v. Mississippi*, it approved the Mississippi plan for depriving Negroes of the franchise. Added to the court-approved legislation that deprived Negroes of rights and freedom was the widespread use of extralegal coercion to keep the Negro "in his place." Lynchings increased drastically during the 1880s, reaching their peak in the early 1890s, when more than 160 Negroes were lynched in one year (Frazier *b*, p. 160).

The motives that led Southern whites to institute new discrimination and that led Northern whites to abandon the Negro are not completely understood. The reaction of Southern whites to military occupation and to the corruption and abuses of the Reconstruction governments may have been partly responsible for the harshness and stringency of discrimination during the post-Reconstruction period. However, some of the more extreme forms of discrimination and segregation were not instituted until twenty or more years after Southern whites regained control of the South, so they could hardly have been a direct reaction to Reconstruction (Woodward, chap. 1). Perhaps Woodward is correct in his belief that increased discrimination against Negroes was largely due to the need for a scapegoat to help reconcile the North and South and to resolve class conflict among whites in the South (chap. 2). In addition, economic incentives to discriminate became greater during the 1880s and 1890s. The educational status of Negroes improved rapidly after 1900 (see Table 1, p. 82), and therefore they became a greater competitive threat. Among the reasons for the abandonment of the Negro by his former white supporters was growing acceptance by Northerners of the doctrine of white superiority. When the United States embarked upon imperialistic adventures toward the end of the nineteenth century, belief in white superiority served as a convenient justification, and Northern and Southern whites became united in their support of white rule.

Whatever the reasons, the Southern Negro by the first decade of the twentieth century was left with only the tag ends of freedom. Most rural Negroes were tenants, and the tenant system frequently resembled economic bondage. Unlike the slave, the Southern Negro of this period had freedom of movement, but this meant little. Industrial jobs in the North were closed to him, and he was usually unaware of opportunities outside his home community. He could neither change the conditions of the South nor escape them. He was buffeted by economic trends and vulnerable to the whims of employers. He adjusted to the world around him instead of acting upon it. He accepted a job as an act of grace instead of bargaining on terms of employment.

The leadership of the period reflected the helplessness of the Southern Negro. Booker T. Washington, principal of Tuskegee Institute and leading Negro spokesman from 1895 through the first decade of the twentieth century, was an "accommodating leader." He accepted the subordinate position of the Negro as an established fact and urged other Negroes to do so. He sought concessions from prominent whites and advised other Negroes to cooperate with and live up to the expectations of whites. A temporizer and compromiser, he sought to ameliorate the problems of Negroes within the existing framework of Negro-white power relations. The salvation of Negroes, he believed, lay in self-improvement, industry, and thrift rather than in equal rights. He eschewed the goal of social equality and, for the immediate future, the goal of economic equality. Negroes could best advance, Washington believed, by concentrating upon being good "hewers of wood and drawers of water." In the famous Atlanta address in 1895, that established him as the white-appointed spokesman of the Negro people, he said: "In all things that are purely social we can be as separate as the fingers, yet one as the hand in all things essential to mutual progress."

Later Washington was considered an "Uncle Tom," and today he is not among the more revered figures in Negro history. His spirit of compromise and conciliation is not in harmony with the spirit of protest of the 1960s, but at the time there was no realistic alternative to his type of leadership. Negroes had practically no resources or opportunities for protest and little support from any segment of the white population. Under the circumstances, vigorous protest activity would have been both futile and dangerous, perhaps suicidal. A few Negroes, mostly in the North, continued to advocate equal rights—for instance, former abolitionist leader Frederick Douglass, until his death in 1895, and later, W.E.B. Du Bois. However, these equal-rights advocates had little influence either upon the Negro masses or upon whites in positions of authority.

From 1900 until World War I, disfranchisement of the Negro continued and became virtually complete in some states, and segregation penetrated the whole society. Not all trends were unfavorable, however. Negro illiteracy declined in the South, and a Negro intelligentsia emerged in the

North that later provided the leadership for effective protest. The National Association for the Advancement of Colored People (NAACP), founded by Negro intellectuals and liberal whites in 1909, adopted a "radical" platform that called for abolition of forced segregation, equal educational opportunities, Negro enfranchisement, and enforcement of the Fourteenth and Fifteenth amendments. Although the NAACP was denounced by most whites who knew of it and by many Negroes, its membership grew rapidly, to 9,500 in 54 branches by 1916 (Frazier *b*, p. 526). World War I and the opening of industrial jobs in the North to Negroes gave major impetus to the drive for equality, and NAACP membership jumped to 88,500 in 1918 with an increase to 300 branches, half of which were in the South. By the end of the war, the downward trend in Negro status had definitely been reversed, although advancement was extremely slow for two more decades.

The conditions of slavery, of the early years of freedom, and of the era of increased segregation shaped Negro social institutions, and certain dominant and persisting characteristics of these institutions conditioned Negro experience during the decades that followed the upturn in Negro status. We turn now to a consideration of the two most important of these institutions, the church and the family.

The Accommodative Negro Church

When slaves were imported to the English colonies in America, their paganism served as justification for the slave status imposed on them, and their white owners were at first hesitant to allow them to be converts to Christianity. At the same time, however, there was reluctance to withhold Christianity from the Negroes. The dilemma was resolved when, in 1667, the Virginia Assembly enacted a law, reaffirmed in 1729 by a declaration of the Crown, stating that baptism in no way altered the status of slaves. This cleared the way for missionary activity among Negroes, and by the time of emancipation, a large percentage of the former slaves were at least nominally Christians.

The first Negro converts became members of predominantly white congregations, but they were never entirely welcome and their participation in religious services was limited. Gradually, most Negroes were segregated into separate congregations, and a few free Negroes withdrew from the white churches and formed separate church bodies. Plantation owners often allowed slaves to conduct their own religious services under close supervision, and the plantation slave preacher emerged as a spokesman who begged the master for favors for his people and in return encouraged docility among the slaves.

After the Civil War, Negroes in the South were expelled from white congregations *and* from white church bodies, and Negro Christians organized their own churches, most of which were variants of the Baptist and Methodist churches. Since the preachers had become established as Negro spokesmen under slavery, and since the church was the only important all-Negro institution at least nominally independent of whites, the church became the most important organization in the Negro community.

The Negro church, in the decades following the Civil War, oriented its members to the dominant white society. Preachers continued to play the mediative roles of Negro spokesmen and representatives of white interests, and the main function of the church in race relations was to accommodate its members to their subordinate status. Efforts of Negro clergymen to work for major changes in the status of Negroes vis-à-vis whites were suppressed on the full restoration of white supremacy during the last decades of the nineteenth century. The freedom of the Negro preacher was circumscribed by the fact that members of his congregation were in debt to whites or dependent upon whites for jobs, and the very land on which the church stood was often the property of whites. The preacher was usually easily controlled, but if other means failed, he could be threatened with violence.

Many, if not most, preachers encouraged acquiescence to white domination, but even without admonitions to "turn the other cheek," the theology and services of the Negro church were conducive to resignation and accommodation. By making inferior status more tolerable, religion lessened incentive to ameliorate that status. The other worldly orientation of the church compensated for the deprivations suffered in this life, and its highly emotional services afforded release from tension and momentary escape from monotony and drudgery. Religion could even subjectively reverse the statuses of the Negro and his white oppressor; the "saved" Negro could feel superior in the eyes of God to the "unsaved" white man. Preachers and lay functionaries found in the church social approval and self-esteem that they could not obtain otherwise. The church further lessened Negro discontent by providing an outlet for energy that otherwise might have been spent in ways troublesome to whites (Glenn *b*).

In spite of its soporific and diversionary influence, the Negro church was not in all ways an obstacle to the improvement of Negro status. Since whites looked upon the church with favor, influential preachers were able at times to gain local concessions and individual favors for Negroes and to mitigate white domination, even though they did not engage in protest activity. The church helped to maintain solidarity in the Negro community and to make possible cautious pressure for improvement in Negro status. Without the church, communication among Negroes would have been based solely on ties of kinship and locality and white-directed activity. The church was an organizational basis with great latent capacity for action, although this capacity was not significantly realized for racial advance for many decades.

The direct control exercised by some whites over Negro clergymen tended to maintain subordination, but this control was not uniformly repressive. Responsible white leaders often communicated with the Negro community through the Negro clergy. They learned of specific needs from the ministers and channeled through them contributions in money or kind for what they judged to be worthy causes. In this way, promising Negro youths were identified and their vocational training fostered, and indigent, sick, or aged persons were assisted. On the other hand, the minister was a convenient device for manipulating numbers of Negroes and for exerting pressure on the Negro population. Warnings and exhortations could be issued from the pulpit, and the minister could be used as an instrument of social control by those interested in maintaining a docile labor force, a group compliant in business transactions and acquiescent to the commands of whites, officials or not. On balance, it seems that the Negro church for most of its history inhibited change and postponed the emergence of an aggressive leadership. When there was agitation for change from other parts of the Negro community, the church was often a conservative force.

The muting of discontent through religion may have had little effect upon Negro status from about 1880 to 1910. Regardless of the strength of Negro discontent, white attitudes and the balance of Negro-white power would probably have permitted little improvement in the status of Negroes. Whether a militant protest movement could have succeeded if the right kind of leadership had been available is a moot point, but Negro preachers could hardly have led such a movement. Semiliterate or illiterate as most of them were, and faced with the tasks of organizing and sustaining the new separate Negro churches, they were ill-equipped to press for major social changes. And, at the local level, there were few if any alternative sources of leadership.

Therefore, the Negro church was as much a reflection of Negro-white relations and the lack of resources of protest among Negroes as a cause of those conditions. Perhaps it is correct to say that "the Negro church fundamentally is an expression of the Negro community itself . . ." (Myrdal, p. 877). However, the Negro church was not merely a malleable, dependent factor in Negro-white relations. Its strong other-worldly orientation and emotional escapism resulted partially from the subordinate status of the Negro, but in turn they reinforced and helped to perpetuate that status.

The foregoing description of the accommodative Negro church characterizes nearly all Southern rural and most Southern urban churches from the Civil War to World War I. Negro churches in the urban North deviated from the accommodative archetype, but they also were generally a conservative force in race relations. Northern clergymen were somewhat better educated than their Southern colleagues, were more independent of white control, and rarely admonished their congregations to be submissive to whites. However, they did not challenge white opinion. Like rural Southern preachers, they were primarily concerned with saving souls.

The Changing Church

After World War I, Negro religion became increasingly differentiated, and it is difficult to enumerate characteristics common to most of the churches. With the great migration of Southern Negroes to the North and the increased cultural and economic differentiation of Negroes, more Negro churches and congregations departed significantly from the accommodative type. Large middle-class and mixed-class Baptist and Methodist congregations grew up in Northern cities. Pastors of these congregations were expected to be "race men," and they devoted much time and energy, as they still do, to advance the race, but, as earlier, their activities did not often go beyond those acceptable to prominent whites. They pursued "welfare" rather than "status" ends (Wilson, p. 185), that is, they were concerned with improving housing, health, education, and morality, rather than with attaining social equality and integration with whites.

By the mid-1940s, only a few Negro clergymen had become "protest" leaders, in the present sense of the term. (Conspicuous among these was Adam Clayton Powell, Jr., pastor of the huge Abyssinian Baptist Church in Harlem, who in 1944 was elected to the U.S. House of Representatives from New York.) Few took the initiative in agitating for full equality of Negroes, but on the other hand, middle-class clergymen in Northern cities were not resistant to change initiated in other quarters. They did not foster an other-worldly escapism among their congregations, but rather were strongly concerned with mundane affairs.

Recently, the role of the Negro church in race relations has changed, although the change has not been uniform among the different kinds of congregations. To the pastors of middle- and mixed-class congregations in the urban North and South alike, being a "race leader" has been redefined as being militantly engaged in seeking full integration of Negroes into American society. Clergymen such as Martin Luther King, Jr., and Ralph Abernathy, among others, have become prominent integrationist leaders in the South. In the North, Negro ministers have provided the leadership for such protest activities as the "selective patronage" movement in Philadelphia. There has been less change in lower-class, storefront sects and rural Southern congregations.

The new role of the Negro church has not been internally generated and spontaneous. Rather it has resulted from a changed mood of the Negro populace and competition from other sources of race leadership and other religious organizations. For some time, the prestige and influence of the Negro clergy have declined, partly because many Negroes have felt that clergymen have not provided positive leadership on behalf of race causes. A large number of professional "race men," the functionaries of such organizations as the NAACP and the National Urban League, have overshadowed the traditional leadership of ministers. Furthermore, the Catholic church, with its espousal of racial equality and integration, has made inroads into the membership of the Negro Protestant churches. Recently, the Nation of Islam ("Black Muslims"), which among other things is a reaction against the "white man's religion" (Christianity), has become in a few Northern cities a serious competitor of the traditional church. Under these conditions, more militancy in racial affairs has become requisite to the continued prominence and growth and perhaps survival of Negro churches.

The Family

The Negro American family differs significantly on the average from the white family, and this difference, unlike many other Negro-white differences, is not essentially the correlate of lower educational and economic status. Rather, it results from the unique background of Negroes and certain distinctive and persistent influences. The experiences of Negroes during slavery and the early years of freedom were especially important in shaping the characteristic features of the Negro family.

Sexual immorality and family instability are among the more prominent features of the Negro stereotype used as justifications by prejudiced whites for rejecting Negroes. Although it has some basis in fact, the stereotype is grossly inaccurate when generally applied, since Negro families now are as varied as white families. However, certain types of families do occur with greater frequency among Negroes. For instance, a large percentage of Negro families are matriarchal or matricentric, that is, the mother is the central figure and main basis for stability and economic support. The relationship between the lower-class Negro mother and the man, to whom she may or may not be married, is insecure and often ephemeral, and the father does not always assume responsibility for the care and support of his children. Marriage, which often is of the common law type, frequently ends in desertion, separation, or divorce. Sex behavior among lower-class Negroes typically is more permissive than that of lower-class whites. Lower-class Negro adolescents usually begin sex relations soon after puberty, and if pregnancy results, marriage is not considered necessary. A premarital pregnancy is considered unfortunate, but the girl is not ostracized nor is her eligibility for marriage greatly impaired (Drake and

Cayton, p. 590). Extramarital affairs are not condoned but they are considered inevitable, and there are no strong sanctions against them.

Negro lower-class sex behavior and family life have their roots in slavery. The social controls that governed sex and family relations among Negroes in Africa were destroyed by the conditions of slavery, and in the absence of new morals and controls, sex relations tended to be casual and promiscuous. Slave owners sometimes encouraged stable relations between men and women and between fathers and their children, but often they did not. Negro males were occasionally used as stallions, and through sales and the division of estates, families were often broken up (Frazier *b*, p. 307). Even when the father remained with his mate and children, the fact that he did not support the family and was as subservient to the master as the others deprived him of strong authority over wife and children. Additional factors making for a mother-centered family were widespread concubinage and transient alliances between white men and Negro women. The white fathers of the children born of such unions were prohibited by convention from playing the role of father, and therefore the mother was necessarily the family head.

Whatever family stability existed among slaves depended to a large extent upon controls exercised by the masters, and therefore the immediate effect of emancipation was an increase in promiscuity and disorganization. Many Negro males used their new freedom of movement to desert their wives and children, and some demoralized mothers abandoned their children. Gradually, new controls emerged and marital stability increased, partly as a result of the efforts of white missionaries and of some Negro churches. The greatest stability was achieved among landowners, who had more reliable means for supporting a family than tenants and laborers. However, the change was slow and was impeded by economic hardship and oppression. Since there was little material reward for self-denial and postponement of gratification, Negroes tended to become hedonistic and pleasure-oriented. Indulgence in sex and alcohol provided momentary relief from drudgery and monotony. Even the religion of rural Negroes was not ascetic or conducive to chastity and family stability. The preachers' frequent denunciation of sin apparently had little effect on the behavior of their congregations, and the preachers themselves were sometimes less than paragons of virtue. The emphasis of religion was upon creating joy rather than upon instilling guilt, and the emotional services were opportunities for expression of impulses rather than restraints on impulsive behavior. The traditional Southern lower-class Negro religion played the opposite role from that ascribed to religion in a Puritanical society (Dollard, p. 249). Instead of stressing self-control and denial of the appetites, this type of religion gave the Negro, through ceremonials that relieved his guilt, poise and freedom to enjoy sensual pleasures.

In contrast to the majority of rural Southern Negroes, many urban descendants of pre-Civil War free Negroes had patriarchal families and stable marital relations. Likewise, the new urban middle class that emerged in the twentieth century is characterized by bourgeois morality and egalitarian or patriarchal families. In fact, some of these middle-class Negroes, in an apparent attempt clearly to distinguish themselves from the lower class, are more Puritanical than their white counterparts. In this respect, as in others, they are extreme examples of middle-class Americans.

However, the sex and family life of lower-class urban Negroes is still similar to that in the rural South. In fact, Frazier says that marital instability and illegitimacy increased as Negroes moved to cities and rural social controls lost their force (Frazier *a*, pp. 630–633). In any event, illegitimacy became a greater problem in the cities. In rural areas mothers without husbands are aided in the care of children by female relatives, and at an early age the children are able to help with chores and contribute to their own support. In contrast, in the city the fatherless child is a great burden, and he suffers greater material and emotional deprivation than he would in the rural neighborhood. With urbanization, illegitimacy became a major obstacle to Negro advancement.

Negro illegitimacy remains high and, according to official statistics, is increasing. In 1961, there were almost 150,000 illegitimate nonwhite births—more than 22 percent of all nonwhite births. This was three times the number of illegitimate nonwhite births in 1940, when the percentage was only 13.7. White illegitimacy also increased from 1940 to 1961, but only from 1.8 percent to 2.5 percent. The nonwhite increase and the divergence of nonwhite and white illegitimacy may not have been as great as these data seem to indicate. In 1961, a greater proportion of Negro children were born in the North, where they were more accurately counted and where greater attention was paid to their paternity than in the rural South. Therefore, more illegitimate Negro children were so identified than in earlier years. Nevertheless, Negro illegitimacy is increasing and is probably increasing more rapidly than white illegitimacy. There are several reasons for this, including a general trend in the United States toward more permissive premarital sex standards. Bearing children out of wedlock still carries stigma among whites, and therefore white illegitimacy has not increased proportionally with increased premarital intercourse. Whites more frequently practice contraception, and if pregnancy does occur, it is more often ended by abortion or made legitimate by marriage. In the absence of strong informal sanctions against illegitimacy in the Negro lower class, more liberal welfare payments for the support of dependent children may, as some critics have charged, lessen the incentive of unmarried women to avoid motherhood. In addition, some couples living together permanently without benefit of clergy may refrain from making their relationship formal merely because marriage would stop or diminish relief payments. It seems unlikely, however, that many unmarried women deliberately bear children for the purpose of receiving welfare payments.

Because of high rates of illegitimacy, divorce, separation, and death, a large percentage of Negro children grow up in fatherless homes. For instance, in 1960, 21 percent of all nonwhite families with children under 18 had female heads, compared with only 6 percent of white families. In many of the homes in which a father or stepfather was present and therefore was classified as the head, he played small part in the support and rearing of the children. The effects upon the child of growing up in a fatherless family are not fully understood, but apparently they are, on balance, detrimental to his chances for educational, economic, and social advancement. He is likely to have to drop out of school to help support the family, and the absence of a father apparently has effects upon the child's personality that hinder achievement. For instance, father-absent children tend to be more submissive and dependent and less willing to forgo immediate gratification for the sake of later rewards (Pettigrew *a*, pp. 17–18).

Illegitimacy and marital instability also hinder advancement by reinforcing negative attitudes of whites toward Negroes. In Northern and Western states with rapidly increasing Negro populations, there is growing concern over mounting costs of welfare payments for the support of dependent Negro children. Objections of taxpayers to high welfare costs often become expressed as anti-Negro sentiments, and Negro immorality—real and imagined—is frequently used to justify continued school and residential segregation.

Traditionally permissive sexual behavior and unstable family life among lower-class Negroes tend to be perpetuated, in turn, by the segregation and discrimination for which they serve as justification. Permissive sex standards are part of the Negro lower-class subculture, and this subculture is reinforced by the segregation and isolation of lower-class Negroes. The inability of many Negro males to find steady and well-paying work undermines their authority in the family and makes them more prone to desert. Sexual indulgence and drunkenness provide respite from a dreary existence of hardship and frustration. A trend in the larger society toward a pleasure-oriented way of life also reinforces the hedonism of lower-class Negroes. Their main contacts with the larger society are through movies and television, which sometimes portray sex standards hardly less permissive than their own.

An additional reason for sexual laxity is a large excess of females in the Negro population. Intense competition for the available males is not conducive to chastity, and in 1960, there were only 89 Negro males for every 100 Negro females in the age range of 15 through 44 years. In contrast, there were 97 white males for every 100 white females. In many large cities, the excess of Negro females was much larger.

The maternal Negro family tends to be perpetuated by the fact that Negro females are, on the average, better educated and therefore are more able to find secure employment than males (see chap. 6). The greater educational attainments of Negro females, in turn, result partly from the tradition of maternal families. Because primary responsibility for family support has resided with the mother, it has been more important for females to have good occupational qualifications, and Negro parents have therefore been more willing to sacrifice for the education of daughters.

Changes in Negro sex and family life will be slow and will depend mainly on growth of the middle class. Growth of the middle class, in turn, depends in large measure upon removal of discrimination and segregation and, especially, upon improved education. There are forces within the Negro lower class that are conducive to family stability, but no marked increase in these forces is likely to occur in the near future. Most lower-class churches to some degree encourage chastity, marital fidelity, and parental responsibility, and the lower-class churches of the cities, unlike those in the rural South, often have a strong ascetic emphasis. The Holiness sects, for instance, strictly forbid drinking, card playing, dancing, and premarital or extramarital sex experience, and known offenders are expelled from the congregations. Baptist churches have standards almost equally stringent, although enforcement is less effective and the doctrine of "once saved always saved" may be conducive to periodic lapses into sin. However, neither the Baptist nor the Holiness organizations have had a great effect upon the family life of urban lower-class Negroes, because their faithful members are mainly women and the cooperation of men is needed to insure marital stability. The general influence of churches in the Negro community apparently has declined in recent years, and it does not seem likely that the churches will soon transform the family life of lower-class Negroes. The Black Muslims apparently have been successful in bringing about marital fidelity and stable, patriarchal families among their adherents, but they have recruited only a minute proportion of the urban Negro lower class.

Since the adoption of middle-class sex standards by lower-class Negroes will necessarily be slow, and since the high illegitimate birth rate is an admitted burden to progress, the proposal to encourage birth control is inevitably raised. Some communities have tentatively initiated programs providing free contraceptive information and supplies to slum dwellers, married and single. However, objections from religious leaders and others to "subsidizing and encouraging immorality" have obstructed this step. Cutting aid-to-dependent-children payments, as proposed by some, would in the long run have effects opposite to the desired ones. A few women might be deterred from giving birth out of wedlock, but it is unlikely that this approach would appreciably affect the birth rate. Since the penalty would fall upon the child as well as the mother and would adversely affect his health and education, any decrease in aid payments would only perpetuate poverty, ignorance, and illegitimacy in future generations. An immediate reduction in illegitimacy seems to depend on the willingness of middle-class whites and Negroes to encourage for others the contraceptive practices they tacitly accept for themselves.

2

A Negro Way of Life

The Negro church, family, and other institutions were shaped by slavery, by the limited freedom that followed, and by segregation and isolation from whites in the South and in the North. Negro life was dominated by the need to adjust to white men and to take them into account at every turn. It was not that the white man was invariably domineering and arbitrary—but he *might* be, and for this the Negro had to be prepared. Consequently, an elaborate and largely one-sided etiquette of race relations grew up in the South (Doyle). The white man took the Negro for granted; the Negro took nothing for granted. The etiquette of Negro adaptation interlocked with and reinforced Jim Crow laws, but it more deeply affected Negroes and Southern life in general because it was informally enforced, because it required overt manifestations of subordination on the part of the Negro rather than mere passive compliance with the law.

Despite the historical uniqueness of the Negro experience, the present state of knowledge does not permit an accurate estimate of the extent to which there is a distinct Negro American way of life, different in kind from that of the surrounding whites. Taken as wholes, the two cultures have far more common than distinctive elements. Over the long run, their convergence would seem to be nearly inevitable. The problem is whether there are cultural differences of sufficient force to affect significantly Negro (and white) adjustment in the difficult years ahead. The differences in the past experiences and present conditions of Negroes and whites suggest that on some important issues they would think, act, and feel differently. One would expect this to be so, even though the differences in experience are often two perspectives of the same experience, two sides of the same coin.

Because Negro life is so much affected by poverty and subservience, it is hard to find distinctive characteristics that can be positively valued. In the stereotype, whatever is admirable in Negro life is assumed to have been adopted from the white man while whatever is reprehensible is assumed to be inherently Negro. This stereotype grudgingly allows the Negro some credit for a primitive musical aptitude, an ability to be cheerful when others would be sad, and a covertly envied capacity for sexual indulgence.

Undeniably, until now, Negroes have made their largest artistic contribution to the common American culture in music, an art form where exceptional talent is rewarded despite lack of formal training.

The Negro's reputed capacity for cheerfulness under stress may contain a germ of truth, although part of the reputation is the result of etiquette—a deliberate effort to put on a happy front for the white man. Certainly, Negroes have been trained in adversity as well as subservience, and many have learned to face the most severe stress with a poise and dignity that is respected in middle-class America. The Negro children who served as the first shock troops for school integration clearly showed such preparation to meet stress, although most of them were probably from middle-class rather than poor families.

High hopes and aspirations for the young are also common values even among the poorest Negroes (Rosen). Realistically channeled, such sentiments can be important spurs for long-run improvements, but the hopes may often be little more than wishes of the desperate, and the means to the desired end may not be well enough understood by the poorest Negroes.

Over and above aspects related to sexual differences, all cultures evaluate men and women differently and emphasize different opportunities for them. Negro American culture seems to value women relatively highly. Considering the strong role of women in the Negro family compared with the white and the emphasis on education of Negro girls, we feel that detailed research would discover further supporting evidence. In this book we must leave the suggestion as conjecture, but if the idea is correct, it presents some interesting problems in connection with leadership within the Negro community and in relations with the white society, which is dominated by men.

Many studies have identified differences on the average in the needs, values, beliefs, and actions of Negroes and whites. But to a great extent, the differences identified are connected with regional and social class differences rather than with the unique Negro condition. In their beliefs and values, Negroes more nearly resemble lower-class than middle-class whites, and whites in the South rather than in the North or West. Many "Negro" traits are also characteristic of poor whites in the rural South.

However, some traits occur much more frequently among Negroes than among whites of similar economic and educational status in the same region. These traits are numerous enough to permit one to distinguish a Negro lower-class subculture, different in important respects from the white lower-class subculture. In a sense, there is also a separate Negro middle-class subculture, although its difference from middle-class white culture is less pronounced.

The full extent of cultural differences between lower-class Negroes and lower-class whites has not been well documented, but insofar as direct measures are possible, most of the differences are small in comparison with those between lower-class and middle-class whites. This is indicated in our analysis of Negro and white responses on some recent public opinion polls (Broom and Glenn). Negro and white responses differed appreciably in almost all of the questions, though when Negroes and whites with similar amounts of education were compared, most of the differences were smaller. The responses of Negroes at each education level tended to resemble those of whites at lower levels. The responses of low-education Negroes were similar to but more extreme than those of low-education whites. For instance, several questions dealt with attitudes toward labor unions: low-education Negroes were consistently more favorable toward unions than were low-education whites, and high-education whites were least favorable. The following percentages said that labor union leaders have too much power.

> Negroes with eight or fewer years of school 27%
> Whites with eight or fewer years of school 49%
> Whites with one or more years of college 72%

In responses concerning the desirability of corporal punishment of juvenile offenders, low-status Negroes differed greatly from whites of both low and high status. The following percentages said that teen-agers who commit serious crimes should be whipped in public:

> Negroes with eight or fewer years of school 52%
> Whites with eight or fewer years of school 17%
> Whites with one or more years of college 15%

The difference between low-education Negroes and whites was so large compared with the difference between low-status and high-status whites that the racial difference could hardly be a simple consequence of educational and socioeconomic differences. However, our comments on a few response patterns only suggest that there are important cultural differences between Negroes and whites in addition to social class and regional differences.

Sex, Family, and Child Rearing

There is substantial evidence that family values and sex standards of lower-class Negroes and whites differ perhaps in kind, and certainly in degree and in the strength of sanctions used to control behavior. The ideal of male dominance and aggressiveness is more prominent among lower-class whites, and the lower-class white family is typically patriarchal. Although sex standards vary within the white lower class, the double standard is typical. Males may engage in premarital and extramarital exploits, but females are expected to remain virginal until marriage and faithful to their husbands after marriage. Infractions of these standards are common, but sex adventures of lower-class white women are more harshly censured and usually are conducted more surreptitiously than are those of lower-class Negroes. Premarital pregnancy brings greater stigma to the lower-class white girl, and she is more likely to try to conceal it.

The child rearing practices of Negroes and whites of comparable educational and socioeconomic status also differ. For instance, a Chicago study reported that Negroes at each status level were more permissive than whites in feeding and weaning children but much more rigorous than whites in toilet training (Davis and Havighurst, p. 710). The same study found that Negroes generally expected their children to assume responsibility at a younger age. In the lower class, Negro fathers disciplined their children more than did white fathers, taught and played with them less, and spent less time with them. In child rearing practices as in most other respects, however, the differences between the lower and the middle classes were greater than the differences between Negroes and whites in each social class.

Religion

Distinctive forms of religious expression constitute an important part of Negro lower-class subculture. Emotional, relatively unorganized church services, with spontaneous singing and shouting by members of the congregation, are now largely restricted to Negroes, although at one time such services were common among rural whites (see Glenn *b*). The preacher's swaying motions and the rhythm that characterizes the singing, preaching, and audience response apparently are uniquely Negro. The services of rural Southern Negro churches appear to a few scholars to bear resemblance to African religious ceremonies, and they judge that there are African survivals in Negro American religion (Herskovits, chap. 7; Simpson and Yinger, pp. 579–581). Although fragments of African religious culture may persist, it seems to us more likely that the religion of Negroes in the United States is primarily the product of experiences on American soil. African religion was heavily dependent on tribal organization, and it is improbable that it survived the conditions of slavery when most other features of African culture did not. The characteristic forms of religious expression of Negro Americans probably grew out of the religious revivals that swept the American frontier starting with the Great Awakening of 1734 and continuing until the last quarter of the nineteenth century. If this is so, the religion of rural Southern Negroes is the evangelical religion of the American frontier, modified to meet the experiences and needs of slaves and freedmen. The frontier brand of evangelical Protestantism has generally disappeared among whites as they have become better educated, more sophisticated, and more prosperous, but it has survived in modified form among Southern rural Negroes, who have been isolated from the mainstream of cultural change and economic advancement.

Money

Negroes and whites with similar incomes allocate their money differently among savings and various kinds of expenditures. For instance, at most income levels Negro families spend less for food, medical care, reading matter, and education, but they spend more than whites for clothing and they save a larger percentage of their income (Alexis; Klein and Mooney). There is a widespread impression among whites that Negroes spend more in relation to their ability to pay for such status symbols as expensive automobiles, fur coats, and jewelry. Negroes at most income levels *do* spend more than comparable-income whites for clothing, but there is no firm evidence that they buy more luxury items. Studies of expenditures have not found that Negroes at any income level spend more than whites for automobile transportation, for example. If, in accordance with widespread belief, a disproportionate number of moderate-income Negroes own luxury automobiles, their high expenditures may be offset statistically by the many Negroes who do not own a car. Or, several young men may jointly buy an expensive car, thus keeping the cost to each rather low (Yoshino, p. 116).

Negro-white variation in expenditures is not necessarily due entirely to cultural differences. Some of it may simply reflect the greater need of Negroes to save. They have lower job security, greater need to prepare for periods of unemployment, and poorer access to sources of credit. More Negroes at given income levels may be nearer their peak earnings, and they may feel a greater pressure to save than whites who anticipate substantial increases in income. However, Negro-white variation in expenditures cannot be fully accounted for on the basis of greater Negro savings; it also reflects differences in values, preferences, and psychological needs.

The tendency of Negroes to scrimp on food and medical care suggests a more urgent need to have money available for display and to provide security against unemployment and other emergencies. Money spent for food and medical care has little display value; it does not compensate for feelings of inferiority that may grow out of whites' negative valuations. Conspicuous consumption is common among persons who are insecure in their status or who feel that their status is not widely recognized. For instance, those who have recently improved their economic standing may buy conspicuously expensive items to communicate the fact that they have "arrived." In contrast, those who have been well off are often rather provident. For them, ostentation would confirm only the obvious, and having come to know money through long intimacy, they prefer not to be separated from it. One would expect more conspicuous consumption among middle- and high-income Negroes than among whites of comparable status, if only because relatively more Negroes have recently moved up from lower-income levels. In addition, the Negro may feel a need to compensate for the fact that his physical appearance symbolizes low status. He knows that his color leads the stranger to assume that he is poor and uneducated, and so he uses other status symbols to demonstrate that this is not true.

Other compensatory behavior probably is more frequent among Negroes than among most categories of whites, though the evidence is tenuous. Negroes probably are more prone than whites to display symbols of their accomplishments, for example, diplomas and Phi Beta Kappa keys and, if entitled to be addressed as "doctor" or by military rank, may be more insistent on the use of the title.

Speech

Negro speech is a distinguishing cultural characteristic (Green, p. 81). Southern Negro dialects, while similar to dialects of Southern rural whites in the same areas, have some distinctive features. Whereas the Northerner may not perceive the difference, persons familiar with the speech of the rural South claim to be able to identify a white or Negro voice without seeing the speaker. Many of the speech and grammatical errors of Southern Negroes are also made by rural Southern whites—both often use double negatives and use "them" as an adjective. But some dialectical variants are more characteristically Negro: for example, "yo" and "sho" for "your" and "sure," and "is" with a plural noun. Even college-educated Southern Negroes—products of the segregated education system—have speech that is often marred with characteristic mispronunciations and grammatical errors. Many Negroes whose grammar is flawless nevertheless speak with an accent that identifies them as Negro, and they, even more than whites with marked regional accents, find their speech a handicap when they move to other regions. Whites with comparable amounts of schooling probably have less regionally distinct accents.

Crime

High rates of Negro crime have caused much concern recently, especially in Northern cities with large Negro ghettos. Official statistics show crime rates to be considerably higher for Negroes than for whites, and the difference is very great in some localities. However, these statistics cannot be taken at face value. The Negro who commits an illegal act is more likely to be arrested, more likely to come to trial, and more likely to be convicted than the white person guilty of the same offense. The Negro in the Deep South is subject to harsher treatment by law-enforcement officials and courts, unless his offense is against another Negro, in which case he may be treated with leniency. Law enforcement outside the South also is often discriminatory. Nevertheless, students of crime and delinquency generally agree that there is a real and not merely a "statistical" difference in the extent to which Negroes and whites commit serious illegal acts.

The reasons for the high Negro crime rate are at least partly cultural. Laws generally reflect middle-class standards and are therefore often at variance with the standards of lower-class Negroes and whites. A larger percentage of Negroes are lower class, and Negro lower-class standards may differ even more than white lower-class standards from the official morality. But even middle-class white conformists regard the police as opponents rather than allies in the support of order and morality. This may be related to the deeply ingrained American mistrust of law, reinforced in recent years by the efforts of otherwise law-abiding citizens to evade the consequences of traffic violations. To an even greater extent, poor Negro adolescents in urban ghettos regard the police as opponents. In their struggles with gangs, the police often fail to distinguish between the casual youthful offense and systematically unlawful behavior. Conflict between police and gangs is all too often characterized by harshly repressive measures and the counteraction that rapidly escalates into continuing violence. When the situation is complicated by race, the cycle of action and counteraction is even harder to interrupt.

Unemployed, economically deprived, and frustrated youth capitalize on opportunities to express their aggressions against their enemies—police and white shopowners. Caught up in the excitement of riots and under the cover of confusion and anonymity, they indulge in looting and the pointless destruction of property. Some of their victims are known and hated by the looters because they will not give credit or hire Negroes or merely because they have desirable merchandise. Others are attacked for no reason other than that they are in the line of march.* Throwing missiles and roaming on rooftops is suggestive of the mock warfare of slum children, and it would be surprising if the combat games of adolescent culture did not find expression during the emotional release of riotous behavior.

Negro organizations have been pressing for increased numbers of Negroes on police forces, and there is merit to their demands. More participation by Negroes in the law-enforcement process could help to modify the Negro's identification of the police as the white man's instrument of repression. The appointment of more Negro officers could help to normalize the occupational distribution and give Negroes a

---

* To the best of our knowledge, there is no study of the selection of economic victims of race riots. Reporters covering the Rochester riot in July 1964 observed, however, that the CORE office, the mosque of the Nation of Islam, and most Negro-owned shops escaped damage.

larger stake in the social order. It may even be argued that Negroes who become peace officers are more highly motivated than the average white, and they may contribute an idealistic leaven to police activity.

On the other hand, the effectiveness of Negro policemen is hampered by the categorical resentment of police in slum areas, a resentment even more aggressively directed against an "Uncle Tom cop" who is viewed as a traitor to his race. The most capable Negro policeman finds his job made more difficult when his racial loyalty comes into conflict with his occupational task, however clear his task may be.

In some lower-class Negro neighborhoods, standards may be evolving that condone violence and predatory activities directed against whites. That there may be an important cultural element behind Negro crime is indicated by recent research that found Negro youths in large Negro population concentrations to be more delinquent on the average than youths of similar economic and social backgrounds in small Negro neighborhoods surrounded by whites (Clark; Clark and Wenninger a, b). It may be inferred that distinctive Negro culture traits have greater strength in large Negro neighborhoods. But other factors, such as crowding and unequal availability of community resources, protective facilities, or even such a simple thing as street lighting, could account for part of the difference in crime rates.

Differences in opportunities to attain goals through legal means are probably more important than cultural backgrounds in accounting for higher rates of Negro crime. Negroes share many goals with whites, and their aspirations are becoming more nearly alike. Yet because of present discrimination and personal limitations that result from past discrimination, Negroes have fewer legitimate opportunities to attain their aspirations, and there is greater temptation to use illegal means. Assimilation of Negroes into the cultural mainstream and their increasing acceptance of commonly held goals may tend to increase criminality unless cultural assimilation is accompanied by a corresponding increase in legitimate opportunities.

High rates of Negro crime may also be related to the conditions of Negro existence which are considerably more frustrating than those of most whites. It is argued that frustration generates hostility, which may be expressed in physical violence. Negro hostility traditionally has been expressed through acts of violence against other Negroes, often against other family members. Negroes in the Old South rarely behaved aggressively against whites, since to do so would have been suicidal, but Negro hostility is now increasingly expressed against whites.

Personality

The few studies that have compared Negro and white personalities have found some interesting differences, but there is little firm knowledge on the topic. A sample of freshmen at a Negro college in the South averaged higher in authoritarianism than a sample of freshmen at a white university in the same town (Smith and Prothro, p. 336). Another study of Negro college students in the Deep South showed them to be, in comparison with white college students, deferent, orderly, submissive, persistent, and with low needs for heterosexuality and exhibition (Brazziel, p. 51). The fact that they were highly deferent and submissive was incongruous with the fact that their needs for aggression were as high as those of white students. A sample of Negro college students in the Upper South had the same general characteristics but differed less from white students. Several studies have shown Negro males to score higher than white males on scales of femininity, and psychotherapists have noted a prevalence of pseudo-masculine defenses among neurotic Negro male patients (Pettigrew *a*, pp. 17–18). Some of these differences may be simply social-class differences, but most of them seem to be the result of the subordinate status of Negroes and of formative years spent in disorganized, fatherless, or weak-father families.

The discrimination that Negroes experience and the prejudice that they perceive tend to lower their self-esteem and cause them to look upon the world as a hostile, threatening place (Pettigrew b, pp. 6–15). The Negro self-image is to a large extent a reflection of the attitudes of whites, and therefore it tends to be a negative image. Negroes have learned to value light skin and other Caucasoid physical features, which have become important bases of Negro social distinctions (Drake and Cayton, pp. 495–506). The widespread use of preparations to lighten skin and straighten hair expresses a Negro devaluation of Negroid physical features. The effects of Negroes' negative self-image and apprehensive view of the world upon other aspects of personality are not well established. For instance, the evidence concerning the relative incidence of mental illness among Negroes and whites is contradictory and inconclusive. However, it is likely that the Negro personality characteristics that develop in response to discrimination and prejudice tend to set Negroes apart from other Americans, lessen their ambition and efficiency, and reinforce negative white attitudes.

Recent developments have enhanced the Negro's self-esteem and mitigated his view of the world as hostile and unfriendly (Pettigrew, b, pp. 6–15). Among the contributing factors are the publicity given to the scientific view that Negroes are not innately inferior, the emergence of the free Negro states in Africa, and the more benevolent policies of the federal and many state governments. Increased self-esteem, in turn, has tended to make the Negro ambitious, more optimistic, and less willing to submit to discrimination, and may lead to a revaluation of racial characteristics.

Probably most cultural and personality differences between Negroes and whites tend to retard Negro advancement. Certain lower-class Negro culture traits, such as permissive sex standards, are a direct hindrance to economic and educational progress, and almost all are indirectly a hin-

drance because whites disparage them and use them as ex-
cuses for continued segregation and discrimination. Engendered as they were of slavery, oppression, and discrimination,
perpetuated as they are by present segregation and discrimination, mocked and derided by whites, the characteristically
Negro traits do not serve as bases of self-respect, *esprit,* or
cohesion.

Continuity and Assimilation

Traits of the Negro lower-class subculture will persist so
long as residential segregation and the accompanying segregation in schools and other institutions persist. This is the
dilemma of official public policy. Many whites do not want to
associate with Negroes, especially not with lower-class ones;
yet segregation of lower-class Negroes merely isolates them
further from the larger society and perpetuates the objectionable lower-class culture. Unless this isolation of Negroes is
broken down, the devalued characteristics of the Negro subculture will harden and expand, thus creating a still greater
problem for future generations. Without segregation and social exclusion, assimilation of Negroes into the mainstream of
American culture would probably be fairly rapid. Negro-
white cultural differences are not so great as the differences
between native Americans and many of the European immigrant populations, and Negroes, unlike some immigrants,
do not have a separate national heritage and do not resist
assimilation. In fact, most of them—excluding only black
nationalists, a few race-proud intellectuals, and the remaining "accommodated" Negroes—strongly desire it, but how
long this attitude will persist depends on whether it is rewarded. The Civil Rights Bill of 1964, if successfully im-
plemented, will strengthen the impulse to cultural assimilation. The drive of many middle-class Negroes to minimize
the differences between themselves and other middle-class
Americans is suggested by their "overconformity" to some
middle-class norms, for instance, in sex behavior, conservatism in dress, and adherence to rules of etiquette.

During recent decades, countervailing influences have tended both to retard and promote Negro assimilation. Desegregation of schools and increased contacts of Negroes and whites on the job have fostered assimilation. Few neighborhoods have been desegregated, however, and as Negro ghettos in cities have expanded, Negro isolation from white society has become more nearly complete. The Negro who lives in the heart of New York's Harlem or Chicago's Black Belt lives in an almost completely Negro world, with only impersonal and stylized contacts with whites on the job and in other economic relations. In a sense, his isolation is greater than that of a Negro in a small town in the South. On the other hand, metropolitan Negroes are more likely to have access to the mainstream of American life, in contrast to Southern Negroes whose contacts are mainly with poor and provincial whites, almost as culturally deprived as themselves. Metropolitan Negroes have more contacts with the mass media of communication, and movies and television may be potent forces for assimilation. As we point out above, however, the mass media may strengthen such lower-class Negro culture traits as permissive sex standards. As more Negroes have advanced to higher educational, occupational, and economic levels, the Negro middle class has become large enough to be a source of cultural change within the Negro community. Lower-class youths in Negro ghettos, who lack virtually all contact with the white middle class, may become imbued with middle-class ideals and aspirations through association with middle-class Negroes. But this depends on the willingness of middle-class Negroes to make themselves available to poorer members of the race with whom they have in common little more than race. Their dilemma is not very different from that of middle-class whites, only more poignant.

On balance, the cultural assimilation of Negro Americans has perhaps accelerated during recent years, and it is a major reason for growing Negro protest. To an increasing extent, Negroes are taking on the values and aspirations of other Americans, and they are demanding the right freely to pursue these goals. Their commitment to American society lies behind their demands for full participation in American life. The initial impetus to the wave of Negro protest of the early 1960s came from the most assimilated segments of the Negro population—college students and other young middle-class Negroes—although now less assimilated people are supporting and engaging in protest.

Negro assimilation has made for increased conflict because the Negro drive for equality, the result of middle-class ideals and aspirations, has not elicited a corresponding white willingness to accede to Negro demands. In the South, the Negro trend toward assimilation may have stiffened white resistance. Southern whites recite lower-class characteristics as reasons for opposing desegregation, but whites, especially lower-class and rural elements, are even more hostile toward assimilated, middle-class Negroes than toward lower-class Negroes who have the traits they claim to deplore. The assimilated middle-class Negro upsets the Southern white's image of what the Negro is; he complicates the racial situation. To many white Southerners, there is an incongruity in a Negro's being ambitious, responsible, self-sufficient, and well dressed. By acting like a member of the white middle-class, he poses a threat to the traditional order and to the economic and psychological advantages of whites.

In other parts of the country, whites have less definite ideas about the place of Negroes in the social order and do not react so negatively to middle-class Negroes. In Northern cities with large Negro populations, some lower-middle-class whites may feel threatened by the ambitions and increasing vocational competence of middle-class Negroes. In general, however, whites outside the South are probably most favorably disposed toward Negroes whose behavior and values are most like their own, and the assimilation of Negroes has probably tended to make them more acceptable to whites as classmates, neighbors, and work associates.

3

Nationalism and Gradualism

Nationalism: Old and New

The historical conditions of the Negro American in many respects have not been conducive to developing a separate nationalism—feelings of group pride and identification with a cultural heritage. Negroes in the United States were largely cut off from their African cultural heritage, and much of their unique culture was born of slavery. They often accepted the white belief in Negro inferiority and came to reject "Negroness."

However, there has been a significant strain of nationalism in Negro American thought. Some Negro nationalists were secessionists, or political nationalists, who advocated the colonization of Africa or the West Indies by Negro Americans. Others were cultural nationalists, who extolled the accomplishments of Negroes, past and present, real and imaginary, and considered the excellence of Negro culture as a reason for full Negro integration into the mainstream of American society. Still others advocated a separate and parallel Negro society within the larger American society.

Negro political nationalism dates from shortly after the

Revolution, when the conditions of free Negroes were deteriorating (Meier). Some free Negroes saw complete withdrawal from American society as the only way to attain the rights, freedom, and opportunities they sought. Advocates of emigration to Africa, and later to Haiti and other places, were numerous among both Negroes and prominent whites. The emigration movements reached their height during the 1850s, when they were characterized by nationalistic feelings and dreams of a glorious past and a glorious destiny for the race. Relatively few Negroes became seriously interested in emigration, however, and fewer yet were able to emigrate. The largest number went to Liberia, which was founded by two white Americans in the 1820s, but even there, residents of Negro American ancestry numbered only about three thousand in the middle of the nineteenth century. By 1925, Americo-Liberians totaled less than twenty thousand out of a population of more than a million.

Cultural nationalism had several major exponents among antebellum Negro writers. These writers did not challenge the legend, then generally believed, that Negroes descended from Ham, one of the sons of Noah. Rather, they gave the story a different twist: Negroes inherited no curse from Ham, they claimed, as proved by the accomplishments and successes of his early descendants—most of the civilized peoples of the ancient world—Ethiopians, Egyptians, Phoenicians, Babylonians, Assyrians, and, through intermarriage, the Hebrews, Greeks, and Romans. Among the descendants of Ham, they asserted, were Moses, David, Solomon, Socrates, Plato, Hannibal, Caesar, Pompey, Jesus Christ, Augustine—a proud array of racial kinsmen.

Later Negro cultural nationalism was more modest in its historical, geographic, and genetic claims, and it emphasized the accomplishments of recent and contemporary Negroes. Out of the later cultural nationalism grew the Association for the Study of Negro Life and History, founded in 1915 by Carter G. Woodson. Woodson exemplified a dualism common among the cultural nationalists—a strong racial pride coupled with a desire for racial harmony and integration.

The first important surge of Negro economic nationalism came with the end of Reconstruction and the desertion of the Negro by many of his white supporters. This period of disfranchisement and increasing segregation is often called the nadir in the history of Negroes in the United States. It then seemed that the only hope for significant advance of the race was through self-help and increased racial solidarity, which were advocated by Booker T. Washington. To Washington, who became the most influential Negro spokesman of the time, the salvation of the Negro lay in thrift, industry, development of manual skills, and cooperation with the "best white men." He suggested that the Jews were worthy of emulation by Negroes (as did Elijah Muhammad a half century later), and he expressed admiration for Jewish unity, pride, and "love of race." He founded the National Negro Business League in 1900 to stimulate Negro business enterprise and advocated exploitation of the Negro market by Negro businessmen and patronage of Negro establishments by Negro consumers. Significantly, Washington advocated the development of separate Negro enterprises to lessen white prejudice and to help incorporate Negroes in American society. However, he never publicly espoused social equality.

Economic nationalism has persisted among Negro businessmen and has received the support of the Negro press and a large number of Northern middle-class Negro clergymen. Twenty years ago and earlier, Negro ministers in Chicago often preached the doctrine of the "Double-Duty Dollar" (Drake and Cayton, pp. 430–433). According to this doctrine, the dollar spent at a Negro-owned store does double service. It buys the desired goods or services and it helps to provide jobs for Negroes. Most Negro consumers, however, have been oblivious to the pleadings of economic nationalists, although with the recent upsurge in race pride and loyalty, more may have become willing to use their buying power to help other Negroes. Negro consumers have generally shopped where they could get the most value for their money, or where credit has been most freely extended, more often than not at white-owned establishments.

THE BACK-TO-AFRICA MOVEMENT

The first Negro nationalist movement with widespread mass support was the "Back-to-Africa" movement led by Marcus Garvey after World War I. Garvey, a Jamaican Negro, came to the United States during the war and organized the Negro Improvement Association in New York. His program was based on the thesis that the Negro would never attain justice and equality in a nation dominated by whites and that Negroes must therefore establish an independent black nation. Garvey idealized the Negro and blackness and disparaged the characteristically white. He organized a uniformed military organization that was to be the nucleus of the army in his new African state, and he created a corps of "Black Cross Nurses." Although his eventual goal was the emigration of Negroes to Africa, he advocated the establishment of a separate Negro economy within the United States as the first step toward complete separation.

At first, Garvey's followers were mostly West Indians, but Southern Negro migrants who flocked into Harlem and other Northern Negro communities eventually added other ears receptive to his doctrine. To many migrants, the North was a Promised Land that failed to live up to expectations. They found race riots, discrimination, and insecure jobs, with none of the paternalistic benevolence of white employers that had often existed in the South. America seemed to be the white man's country, as Garvey claimed. Garvey offered the disillusioned masses from the South a new Utopia, an independent Negro nation in Africa. And they responded by the thousands, in New York, in Chicago, in Philadelphia, and in Detroit.

As popular as Garvey's movement was for a time, not a single Negro American emigrated to Africa as the direct result of his efforts. In an overzealous attempt to finance a fleet of steamships to carry Negroes to Africa, Garvey ran afoul of federal law, was convicted of using the mails to defraud, and was sent to the federal penitentiary in Atlanta. He continued to direct his movement from prison, but without his presence it declined. A few Garveyites are still to be found in Northern cities, but most Negro nationalists long ago turned to other movements.

THE BLACK MUSLIMS

Small black nationalist organizations that have attracted ex-Garveyites and like-minded individuals have been numerous since the Back-to-Africa movement. Most have gained only a small following, but one, after nearly two and a half decades of near oblivion, has burgeoned into a mass movement perhaps comparable to the Garvey movement. This is the Nation of Islam, commonly known after C. Eric Lincoln as the Black Muslims (Lincoln; Essien-Udom).

Less than a decade ago, few Negroes and fewer whites had heard of this organization; today, few have not. But the rise of the Black Muslims themselves has not been so explosive as the increase in publicity about them. Newspaper and popular magazine accounts probably give an exaggerated impression of Muslim strength, militancy, and importance in the transformation of the Negro American. Yet the movement is highly significant, if only because it has dramatized the Negro "problem" for many whites and because it has mobilized and sensitized Negroes at the lowest economic level—Negroes who were little influenced by established betterment associations.

The founder of the Black Muslims (who, incidentally, are not recognized by the orthodox Moslem community in the United States) was W. D. Fard, a mysterious peddler, perhaps an Arab, who appeared in Detroit in the early 1930s. As he went from house to house, he told Negroes of their homeland across the sea and proclaimed himself a prophet who had come to awaken the Black Nation to its possibilities in a world temporarily dominated by whites. He exhorted Negroes to stop imitating the evil ways of whites, to renounce the white man's religion, and to worship Allah, the *one* true God.

As mysteriously as he appeared, Fard disappeared in 1934, leaving some 8,000 followers. His chief lieutenant, Elijah Muhammad (formerly Elijah Poole), assumed leadership and moved the group's headquarters from Detroit to Chicago. Under Elijah, membership at first declined, and the survival of the sect seemed in doubt when many of its adherents were imprisoned during World War II for refusal to serve in the Armed Forces. However, Elijah's following increased slowly after the war, and by the late 1950s the movement was flourishing. In 1959, a rash of newspaper and magazine accounts of the Muslims appeared, and this publicity further stimulated Muslim growth. One estimate, probably exaggerated, is that membership doubled within six months. By 1961 there were at least 50 Muslim temples and missions from New England to California and Florida, and membership was estimated at 100,000. Observers report that Muslim growth in the Chicago Southside continues to be rapid and that for each Muslim in good standing there are perhaps two or three others sympathetic to and influenced by the movement. However, no well-based estimate of current membership is available.

The Muslims are extreme nationalists. To them, "so-called Negroes" are in all ways superior to whites. According to Muslim mythology of racial origins, all men originally were black. But within each black man there were two elements— the black, which contained all virtues and strengths of man, and the white, which contained all evils and weaknesses. A scientist separated the white from the black and thus created the white race. These "blue-eyed devils" were given 6,000 years by Allah to rule the earth, plus a 70-year grace period during which the Black Nation is to be awakened. The period of grace is to expire in "1984." [*sic!*]

Because of their belief in black superiority, Muslims oppose interracial social relations and marriage, much as do proponents of white supremacy. Integration of "so-called Negroes" with whites they consider degrading. The Muslim goal is complete separation of blacks from whites, first socially, then economically, and finally politically. Immediate severing of all social relations with whites is enjoined, and good Muslims do not seek the friendship even of Christian Negroes. As a step toward a separate Negro economy, the Muslim organization has founded business enterprises, mainly retail and service establishments, that are patronized by all good Muslims regardless of price, quality of merchandise, or credit terms offered by white competitors.

Political and geographical separation is to be attained by setting aside a large area of the United States for the exclusive use of blacks. As an alternative, Elijah has hinted that blacks might settle for emigration to Africa, although at another time he said that America rightfully belongs to the blacks and that the whites should go back to Europe. The goal of political independence is ill-defined, or at least public statements by Muslim leaders have been vague and somewhat inconsistent.

The early Muslims were chiefly poorly educated Negroes from the rural South. Most adherents still are recruited from the economically depressed segments of the Negro population, but more now have urban backgrounds. A small but increasing number of college students and other middle-class Negroes have joined the movement. Although well-educated Negroes cannot accept the more naïve elements in the ideology and mythology, Muslim sympathizers appear to be fairly numerous among Negro college students in Northern universities. Muslim members typically are young, an estimated 80 percent being between the ages of 17 and 35. Men outnumber women, the reverse of the situation in Christian churches. Many adherents are former criminals, prostitutes, and narcotic addicts, and all remain reformed as long as they remain in the movement. The apparent success of the Muslims at rehabilitating such deviates has not been carefully investigated, but it may be greater than the success of agencies and organizations that have rehabilitation as a primary purpose.

The appeal of the Muslims to the lower-class Negro is not hard to understand. Participation in the movement gives him a feeling of self-respect, of superiority, of identification with a cause. Instead of waiting decades to attain equality with the white man, he can be superior now. However, the reasons for the accelerated growth of the movement in recent years are not so readily apparent. Why were not urban lower-class Negroes so susceptible to the Muslim appeal ten, fifteen, or twenty years ago? In the 1940s and late 1950s, as in the 1920s when the Garvey movement flourished, the Northern cities turned out to be a disappointing Promised Land to many Negro migrants from the South. During World War II and the Korean conflict, jobs were numerous and pay was good in Northern industry, and Negroes flocked northward by the thousands. By the late 1950s, however, an economic recession and the trend toward the elimination of unskilled work by mechanization left a large percentage of poorly educated Negroes from the South unemployed.

The decade of the fifties was, to be sure, a period of numerous court decisions and pronouncements favoring the Negro. Mass media were filled with reports of agitation and debate in the field of civil rights. Increased support of Negro equality by the courts, by high officials in the federal administration, by prominent white organizations, and by upper- and middle-class Negroes strengthened and gave legal sanction to the view that Negroes deserved a better lot in American society. And yet the objective lot of lower-class Negroes changed little, and in some cases deteriorated. They faced the same discrimination, the same rejection by whites and by upper- and middle-class Negroes, the same difficulty in getting and keeping jobs. Perhaps many lower-class Negroes in the ghettos of the North realized that even the most vigorous efforts—official or nonofficial—toward integration could help them little in the near future. On the other hand, the psychological rewards of being a Muslim were immediate, and even the tangible gains that came from Muslim asceticism and self-improvement were more perceptible than the benefits that accrued to them through efforts of integrationists.

Such nationalistic movements as Garveyism and the Muslims have thrived mainly in cities outside the South, since disillusionment with integrationist goals is most prevalent where there is the greatest discrepancy between practice and generally accepted ideals of racial equality. In the South, where racial equality is neither the general ideal nor the practice, Negroes have had little reason to be disillusioned with the integrationist approach, which until quite recently had not been tried.

How prominent Negro nationalism will be in the future depends largely upon how successful integrationists are in satisfying the aspirations of all classes of Negroes. Nationalism probably will remain an important influence on integrationist leaders and organizations and on their relations with the white leadership. Faced with competition from the Muslims, the integrationists have been forced to be more militant and bold in order to win support from the urban Negro masses. They have also used the "Muslim threat" as a weapon for gaining concessions from white leadership. The NAACP, once considered radical by many conservative white leaders in the North (and South), now appears moderate when compared with the Muslims. Perhaps as a consequence, many white leaders have become more willing to accept the NAACP and other integrationist organizations as bargaining agents for the Negro community. Failure to do so, they correctly perceive, would strengthen the position of the extremists.

Gradualism, Self-Improvement, and Welfare Goals

Black nationalism has never been a dominant theme in Negro American life, but until recently neither was the militant and urgent drive for full integration into American society. From the late nineteenth century until World War II, the predominant orientation of Negroes, both leaders and masses, was moderate and adaptive. Most did not want to migrate to an unknown and remote Africa, nor did they want greater social and economic separation of the races within American society. Many were "integrationists" in the sense that they hoped for the eventual elimination of at least some forms of segregation, but desegregation was not an urgent goal that most Southern and Border Negroes hoped to attain quickly. Because they did not expect rapid change in Southern institutions, Negroes adapted as well as they could and sought improvement of their lot within the framework of segregation. But acceptance of the status quo was never as complete as many Southern whites believed: most Negroes did not reveal their aspirations and their objections to segregation because apparent compliance served their immediate and attainable goals. Almost all Negroes were in some way dependent upon whites—for employment, for tenure on the land, for credit, for legal guidance, for political intercession, for personal charity, for some kind of assistance. They had much to lose by overt and challenging protests that might alienate or embarrass white sponsors—even the most sympathetic ones—and would only antagonize whites with whom more formal business relations were conducted. In the face of overwhelming power, Negroes were moderate in what they asked and compliant before the acts, decisions, and values of whites.

Throughout this period, a number of Negroes did openly work for desegregation, in the South as well as in the North, but their activities were the exception rather than the rule. From its founding in 1909, the NAACP espoused and worked for integrationist goals, but until the last two decades its membership was almost entirely middle-class, and it received little support, financial or otherwise, from the majority of Negroes. Even many local functionaries and members of the NAACP were more concerned with "welfare" than with "status" ends (Wilson, p. 185). That is, they were primarily concerned with better Negro schools, better pay and working conditions in "Negro jobs," improved public and private welfare services for Negroes, and other changes that would help the Negro's condition though leaving intact segregation and subordination.

The patience of Negroes and the relative lack of militant agitation for change during the first four decades of this century are not difficult to understand. The burdens of day-to-day existence, the problems of getting food and shelter and providing for basic needs—these so absorbed their attention that they had relatively little concern for social equality. In other words, their welfare needs were so urgent that they were often scarcely aware of their status needs. Furthermore, people generally aspire only to goals that seem possible of attainment; white resistance to change was so great, and Negro resources for protest so scant, that hope for immediate rapid change in the segregated pattern simply was not realistic. The paucity of Negro resources for protest was a decisive obstacle to change. From 1914 through 1936, only about 32,000 academic and professional degrees were granted to Negroes and most of these by inferior Negro colleges (Johnson, p. 9). Of the Negro college graduates, who were best qualified to be leaders of protest, a large percentage were employed by Negro institutions and were not strongly inclined to protest against segregation. The Negro white-collar class, from which protest leadership and impetus later came, was very small and increased but slowly before 1940. White-collar workers comprised not more than about 3 percent of the employed Negro labor force in 1910 and only about 6 percent in 1940, and most of these served in the semiseparate Negro economy and therefore had a stake in the status quo. A sizable Negro middle class employed in the integrated economy did not emerge until World War II.

During the Great Depression of the 1930s especially, the economic needs of Negroes were so urgent that they took precedence over any other aspirations. During this decade, membership of the NAACP declined and the interest of the

Negro masses in such abstract goals as social equality fell to an even lower level than in the 1920s. It was at this time that the Communist party made its greatest inroads among Negroes (Record *a*). The Communist ideology, with its emphasis upon the economic exploitation of the masses, was more directly relevant to the urgent needs of unemployed and poverty-stricken Negroes than was the integrationist program of the NAACP. Surprisingly, however, relatively few Negroes embraced communism. The proportion of American Communist party members who were Negro was probably never much more than about 10 percent—approximately the proportion of Negroes in the total U.S. population (Logan, p. 82). The communists alienated many Negroes by advocating segregation of Negroes into a forty-ninth state, and they gained few Negro adherents later by shifting to a policy of integration. The labor movement and the welfare programs of the New Deal were more appealing to most Negroes, not only because they conflicted less with traditional values and loyalties but also because they were able to deliver immediate benefits.

Although most Negroes probably preferred integration to separate development of Negro institutions, during the 1920s and 1930s there was still widespread hope that Negro institutions and facilities could be truly equal even if separate, and this hope tended to lessen aspirations for integration. Only after another decade of futile striving for equality was this hope largely dispelled among Negro leaders. By the 1940s, the decline of small business in the United States was well under way, and it became apparent that the fledgling semi-separate Negro economy would never reach maturity. The Southern and Border states continued to refuse equal financial support to Negro schools and colleges. At the same time, social science research and opinion crystallized around the conviction that segregation was damaging to Negroes and, in the long run, to the society as a whole. Prominent social scientists, such as E. Franklin Frazier and Gunnar Myrdal, and many quieter voices in college classrooms, argued with increasing force and with growing numbers of listeners that many Negro institutions, including schools and businesses, could never be more than mediocre imitations of white ones. The integration movement came of age during the forties, and the doctrine of "separate but equal" became one of the Negro "faiths that failed" (Lomax, chap. 4) .

Negro gains during the period of gradualism and self-improvement before World War II were small relative to later gains, but nevertheless they were important. Certain kinds of Negro businesses, such as insurance companies, cosmetic manufacturing companies, and funeral parlors, became moderately prosperous. Growing concentrations of Negroes in Northern cities opened opportunities for Negroes in politics, and in 1928 the first Negro congressman since Reconstruction, Oscar de Priest of Chicago, was elected. Other Negroes were elected to state and local offices. Enrollments in Negro colleges grew, thus creating positions for Negro professors and administrators. The Negro press thrived, taking advantage of the unique needs and interests of Negroes that resulted from their isolation and segregation. Negro professional organizations were founded or increased in size and importance, and these provided many Negroes with opportunities for participation, recognition, and practice in coping with organizational machinery and with problems in human relations.

Ironically, many of the Negro gains that occurred in the context of segregation now tend to inhibit integration and thereby to lessen long-range chances for Negro advancement. These gains created a large body of Negroes who benefit in one way or another from segregation and who therefore are less than fully committed to the goal of integration. The teacher, the college administrator, the publisher, the businessman, the politician, the clergyman, the officer of a Negro professional organization—all stand to lose in some way from desegregation. The prospect of loss is very remote for some, such as the publisher and the clergyman, and therefore it is not likely to inhibit greatly their efforts for integration, at least not for the time being. For others, such as teachers in all-Negro schools in Border states, the prospect of loss is immediate, and they are often reluctant supporters of integration. Some for whom the actual loss is slight, perhaps only psychological, do not enthusiastically embrace integration. For instance, separate medical societies are sometimes maintained after the predominantly white societies admit Negroes because Negro doctors can more easily win recognition in their own organizations.

To return to the period of gradualism, it was one of isolation from the mainstream of American life. The dominant emphasis of both Negroes and whites who sought Negro progress was upon self-improvement and the development of separate businesses, institutions, and organizations. Negro businessmen were encouraged to take advantage of the protection offered by segregation, and they tried to do so. In attempts to overcome the detriments of their exclusion from white organizations, Negroes formed separate professional organizations. The Negro press and, in the North, Negro politicians exploited special Negro interests and concerns. And yet, for all the emphasis on separate and parallel institutions, there was no pervasive spirit of true Negro nationalism. A few Negro businessmen, clergymen, and leaders looked upon the development of a separate economy as a permanent solution to Negro economic ills, but most Negroes did not share their faith. Even many Negroes who actively worked for the development of separate institutions did not regard them as permanent but rather as stopgap measures, preparatory to integration. Like Booker T. Washington, they thought that Negroes could best demonstrate their readiness for integration by successfully operating their own businesses and organizations. Furthermore, most Negroes lacked the pride and group identification that characterize true nationalism. Few shared Carter G. Woodson's pride in and enthusiasm for Negro culture and history. The emphasis upon Negro institutions did not grow out of a general preference for separate institutions but rather out of lack of realistic alternatives. If Negroes were to advance at all, it seemed that it had to be along the only route open to them—a separate route. That route was a dead-end street, as many Negroes could see, but movement toward a dead end seemed better than no movement at all.

The emphasis on Negro self-improvement, which was started by Booker T. Washington and lasted until World War II, was ill-timed and yielded only meager dividends. Well-educated, well-qualified Negroes could not hope to find employment where they could make full use of their capabilities. It was not uncommon for Negro college graduates to be employed as baggage porters or dishwashers or in other kinds of menial work. Southern Negroes who showed more than the permissible amount of ambition, resourcefulness, and industry elicited the epithet of "uppity nigger" and were sometimes subjected to harassment and physical mistreatment because they did not "know their place."

The impulse for self-improvement was supported by several different forces. First, as we have observed, Negro leaders saw self-improvement as a demonstration exercise to convince whites that Negroes deserved increased opportunities. Many sincere whites agreed that reward should follow proof of virtue, and many of these people encouraged attitudes of self-help, fostered individual Negroes, and assisted Negro educational and helping agencies. Other Negroes felt that the only hope for betterment was self-help of a sort that would not generate conflict. In addition, there was a pervasive attitude in parts of white America that denied Negroes had been held back and blamed their inherent weakness for their poverty and low status. This point of view absolved whites of responsibility and increased their self-righteousness, while it placed blame on the shoulders of those who could not shrug it off. Accommodating Negro leaders, including Booker T. Washington and Southern Negro preachers, helped to instill self-blame in Negroes, encouraging the view that their sorry plight was at least partly their own fault. But self-blame motivated neither self-improvement nor aggressive action.

Since efforts at self-improvement brought little tangible reward, they led to feelings of frustration and eventually to atrophy of interest in self-improvement.

The pendulum has now swung away from self-blame and self-improvement. Most Negroes today blame their plight upon the white man. If one accepts the view, now almost universally held by social scientists, that biological differences between Negroes and whites are in no important way responsible for differences in culture, personality, and social structure, then it follows that the white man *is* ultimately responsible for the social and cultural characteristics of the Negro American. White men brought Negroes to the New World, destroyed their African social organization, cut them off from their African cultural heritage, completely controlled the conditions of their existence during slavery, and almost as completely determined their conditions after emancipation. Negroes gained their freedom because of a falling out among white men and lost much of their freedom a few decades later because of a reconciliation of white men (Woodward, p. 53). Since then, Negroes have advanced only when and where and under conditions allowed by white men. In a very real sense, the Negro American was created by the white man. When the white man views the Negro, he looks upon his own handiwork and that of his forebears. Now the Negro is insisting that he be allowed to remake himself without historical impediments, or with help where there used to be hindrance, or that he be compensated for being what he has been made.

The Negro's belief that he is what the white man has made him is correct, but like many correct beliefs it is not entirely beneficial to those who hold it. Many Negroes fail to distinguish between the effects of earlier discrimination, which is responsible for present Negro shortcomings, and the effects of present discrimination. Quite naturally, they tend to take advantage of one of the few benefits of minority status, namely, the fact that discrimination rather than personal limitations can be conveniently blamed for failures and troubles. The tendency to use this excuse becomes stronger as more publicity and attention are given to discrimination. Regardless of whether Negro troubles result from present discrimination or Negro shortcomings that grew out of past abuses, whites are at fault. But from the standpoint of civil rights strategy, the distinction is of vital importance. If Negro problems are caused primarily by present discrimination, then action to reduce discrimination should have the highest priority. If, on the other hand, Negro shortcomings are primarily to blame, massive efforts at self-improvement, necessarily with white assistance and cooperation, are needed. In most cases, both discrimination and Negro weaknesses are at fault, and so a two-pronged strategy of uplift and protest should be most effective. Negro organizations now emphasize both self-improvement and attacks upon discrimination, the National Urban League giving the greatest attention to the former. Overall, however, Negro strategy is now weighted on the side of protest. Partly as a consequence of this emphasis, discrimination, especially in employment, is diminishing somewhat more rapidly than Negroes are becoming prepared to take advantage of the new opportunities. (Present and recent discrimination in education is, of course, one reason why Negroes are not better prepared for new job opportunities.) The self-improvement emphasis, although ineffective during the early decades of this century, would now be consonant with opportunities for Negro advancement.

4

Action and Integration

Government Policy and the Shift in Negro Goals

Present Negro demands for integration in schools, housing, and public facilities have dramatic urgency. Feelings of discontent and frustration were carried for decades as psychological burdens, and they could be expressed safely only in the most tentative and veiled fashion. With apparent suddenness, it has become permissible to express discontent, to lay blame on the white man, and to seek redress. To be sure, in some places this can be hazardous, but overt protest and open demands increasingly characterize the organizational strategy and the personal attitudes of Negro Americans. The shift in goals from "separate but equal" to integration has permeated even the rural areas of the Southern "Black Belt," where thousands of Negroes have shown themselves willing and able to respond to integrationist appeals. It is there, of course, that the change has been less complete; many elderly and poorly educated Negroes, trained to subordination and fearful of reprisal, remain unwilling to change their accustomed ways. For instance, in some areas, voter registration drives have had little success. Overall, however, the shift has been dramatic, and it has been surprisingly inclusive of Negroes in different localities and of different circumstances.

The change to the new outlook has been erratic and has resulted from numerous forces. There have been periods of drift, as in the early 1930s, and periods of very rapid shifts in the prevailing goals of Negroes, as during World War II, the months following the 1954 school desegregation decision by the United States Supreme Court, and the early 1960s. The underlying factors include urbanization of Negroes, the increase in the number of educated Negroes, the growth of a middle class, the assimilation of Negroes into the cultural mainstream, and the conspicuous failure of separate facilities to become equal.

A crucial reason for—and, to some extent, a consequence of—increased demands for integration is the changing legal interpretation of segregation. In part, the changed outlook of the Supreme Court reflects "cultural drift" toward more egalitarian values in the United States. Although the rulings of the Court are not necessarily a direct reflection of prevailing views among the populace, changes in the philosophy of the Court occur in the context of and more or less in harmony with broader cultural and social trends. The Court is not vulnerable to direct political pressures, but political considerations influence appointments to the Court, and therefore the balance of influence among interest groups has some bearing on the Court's makeup. Efforts of the NAACP and NAACP Legal Defense and Education Fund to bring segregation cases before the Court have been necessary, but they are certainly not sufficient to account for the Court's reversal of earlier rulings that favored segregation.

Whatever their reasons, the Supreme Court's rulings have greatly intensified the Negro's striving for integration. They have made integration the "law of the land" and have given the drive for equality the stamp of legitimacy. They have tended to dispel doubts about the rightness and justice of integration and have made Negroes more indignant about and resentful of remaining segregation. They have instructed Negroes that overt and forceful action through formal and recognized channels might be rewarded rather than punished.

The Supreme Court's support of integration is recent. During the latter part of the nineteenth century, when popular opinion was against Negro rights, the Court added its weight to forces that relegated Negroes to second-class citizenship. In the *Civil Rights Cases* of 1883, the Court held that the Fourteenth Amendment gave Congress power to restrain states but not individuals from acts of racial discrimination and segregation, and thus it effectively nullified the restrictive parts of the Civil Rights Act passed during Reconstruction. In *Hall v. de Cuir* (1877), the Court ruled that a state could not prohibit segregation on a common carrier, and in *Louisville, New Orleans, & Texas Railroad v. Mississippi* (1890), it ruled that a state could constitutionally *require* segregation on carriers. In *Plessy v. Ferguson* (1896), the Court established the "separate but equal" rule that prevailed for more than half a century, basing the decision on the doctrine that "legislation is powerless to eradicate racial instincts."

In 1915, the tide turned in favor of Negroes when, in *Guinn and Beal v. United States,* the Supreme Court for the first time struck down one of the disfranchising devices of a Southern state. The Louisiana "Grandfather Clause," which exempted from voting requirements persons whose ancestors had voted prior to January 1, 1867 (the requirements thus were imposed almost exclusively upon Negroes), was held to be in violation of the Fifteenth Amendment. However, the next major decision concerning Negro rights did not come until 1935 when, in *Norris v. Alabama,* systematic exclusion of Negroes from juries was ruled to be *prima facie* evidence of denial of equal protection under the law as guaranteed by the Fourteenth Amendment. And not until 1944 was there another major ruling in favor of Negro voting rights: in

Smith v. Allwright the Court decided that refusal of the Democratic party of Texas to permit Negroes to vote in its primary was a violation of the Fifteenth Amendment.

The Court's attack on legalized segregation did not begin suddenly in 1954 with the school desegregation decision in *Brown v. Board of Education of Topeka*. The first major ruling on exclusion of Negroes from educational institutions was the Gaines case in 1938 (*Missouri* ex rel. *Gaines v. Canada*), in which the Court decreed that Missouri had to admit a Negro to its state university law school because providing a scholarship to attend school in another state did not meet the requirement for equal facilities. In a series of decisions between 1941 and 1950, the Court forbade segregation on trains engaged in interstate commerce. In 1950, the Court ruled in *Sweatt v. Painter* that the University of Texas Law School must admit a Negro applicant because a hastily improvised separate law school did not offer equal facilities or substantially equal opportunities for legal training. On the same day, the Court ruled that a Negro admitted to the University of Oklahoma Graduate School was denied equal protection under the Fourteenth Amendment because he was segregated from white students in the library, cafeteria, and classrooms. Partly as a result of these two decisions, desegregation of graduate and professional schools in several Border and Southern states was already well along when the 1954 decision ordered desegregation at the lower levels of the educational system.

As important as the earlier decisions were, none had so great an effect upon Negro outlook as the decision of May 17, 1954. Most Negroes probably knew little or nothing of the earlier decisions, but within a few weeks after the Court ruled that separate Negro schools are inherently unequal, almost every adult Negro was at least vaguely aware of the substance of the decision and sensed its importance. The publicity and commentary that followed the decision, and especially the consternation it caused Southern whites, communicated even to the most unsophisticated Negro that the decision augured great changes. Although there was no immediate improvement in their objective status, the pronouncement of the nation's highest tribunal created a feeling of "first classness" among Negroes. It increased aspirations and expectations. In the long run, the decision also tended to increase frustration and restiveness, since for the vast majority of Negroes there were no tangible benefits. However, even those who did not care about sending their children to school with whites and who had little concern with the direct consequences of enforcement of the decision were given a greater feeling of self-respect and hope for the future.

Civil rights legislation and executive orders barring discrimination have largely been a result of Negro demands, and in turn they have reinforced Negro desire for equality. Until the Civil Rights Bill was signed into law July 2, 1964, civil rights legislation was largely confined to the state and municipal level. During the postwar period, many Northern and Western states and cities passed legislation barring discrimination in public accommodations or in employment. The effects of this legislation on Negro attitudes are not clear and probably vary among different classes of Negroes. The tangible benefits have accrued largely to the middle class who can afford to travel and patronize hotels and restaurants and who have the necessary qualifications to take advantage of lessened job discrimination.

It would be inaccurate to say that antidiscrimination legislation has increased the dissatisfaction of middle-class Negroes, because when the law is enforced they appreciate its benefits. But it probably has whetted their appetites for additional gains, made them more impatient with remaining discrimination, and spurred them to intensify their drive for equality. Lower-class Negroes, on the other hand, have gained little. They cannot afford to use many of the public facilities that have been opened and they are not qualified for most jobs from which the race bar has been lowered. Legislation has not solved their most basic and pressing problems, and to the extent they had expected it to do so, they are disillusioned. Their problems result not so much from the present discrimination that legislation prohibits as from the accumulated effects of centuries of subordination and under-privileged existence. "Pro-Negro" legislation may give them a temporary psychological lift, but it may also leave them disappointed. Some, disillusioned with the goal of integration, have turned to the Black Muslims and other nationalist movements. Others place their hope in more complete integration for benefits it will bring their children and grand-children, if not themselves. Some, perhaps a majority, of lower-class Negroes have only vaguely defined goals and ideas about the action they should take to better their lot. Many participate in protest activity not because the ostensible goals of the activity have much meaning to them, but because participation provides an outlet for restlessness and hostility against whites.

Executive Orders from the White House have even more clearly increased the urgency of Negro demands for equality and integration. In June 1941, A. Philip Randolph, president of the Brotherhood of Sleeping Car Porters, threatened a march on Washington by Negroes to obtain better job opportunities. As a result, President Roosevelt issued Executive Order 8802, which forbade discrimination by holders of government war contracts. The order contributed significantly to the substantial Negro occupational gains of World War II. As we point out in Chapter 6, these occupational gains in turn heightened Negro desire for full participation in American life. Executive Order 9981, issued by President Truman in July 1948, had perhaps an even greater effect on the outlook and aspirations of Negroes. The order stated that "there shall be equality of treatment and opportunity for all persons in the armed services without regard to race, color, religion, or national origin." By the mid-1950s desegregation of the Armed Forces was complete, except in the Reserve Officers' Training Corps (in which remaining segregation was based upon segregation in colleges and universities) and the National Guard. Thousands of Southern Negroes have served in integrated military units and, at least on the surface, have been accorded the same treatment as whites of the same rank. Many have risen to positions of authority over whites. The soldier who experiences such equality is not likely to return docilely to the role of the servile Southern Negro who "knows his place" and is content to stay there.

The Role of the NAACP

The shift of the majority of Negroes to integrationist goals and the transformation in their aspirations must be attributed in large part to the National Association for the Advancement of Colored People. Hated by Southern white conservatives and admired by most Negroes and white liberals, the NAACP is one of the most controversial, influential, and highly publicized American organizations of the twentieth century. Founded in 1909 by a small group of white humanitarians and liberals and young Negro intellectuals—among them Jane Addams, William Dean Howells, John Dewey, Oswald Garrison Villard, Mary White Ovington, and W. E. B. Du Bois—it was for nearly three decades a relatively insecure organization whose very survival was often in doubt. Nevertheless, during its early years it initiated action that led to several important Supreme Court decisions, including the epochal decision in *Guinn and Beal v. United States* in 1915. Almost every subsequent civil rights case was brought before the Court through the efforts of the NAACP or, after 1939, the NAACP Legal Defense and Education Fund, a separate organization set up to afford tax exemptions to contributors.

Although it is highly regarded by the Negro populace, the NAACP is not a mass organization that is guided by the views of the majority of Negroes. It has not ignored lower-class Negroes, but its understanding of their needs has not always coincided with the views of the lower-class Negroes. From its beginning, the NAACP has concentrated on action through the courts, although it has also tried to influence legislation and has employed various pressure group methods. It maintains a centralized organization controlled from the national headquarters, a feature that strengthened its resistance to communist attempts at infiltration during the 1930s (Record *a*). Major action is taken at the national level, with local chapters being often not much more than dues-collecting agencies for the national organization. Although the chapters are permitted, and in fact encouraged, to engage in local action if their techniques are acceptable, the national office generally does not instigate nor direct such action. However, the national organizations of both the NAACP and NAACP Legal Defense and Education Fund support and occasionally instigate local suits to challenge segregation and discrimination, and the national office of the NAACP presses for local implementation of state and federal court rulings and legislation favorable to Negro rights. In such cases, however, the local action is deemed to be of national significance.

During the late 1930s and early 1940s, the NAACP was one of three almost equally prominent and influential organizations that pressed for Negro rights. The other two were the National Urban League, founded only two years after the NAACP, and A. Philip Randolph's Brotherhood of Sleeping Car Porters. During the 1940s and early 1950s, the NAACP eclipsed the others, largely because it won a series of important court decisions that nullified restrictive covenants, gave Negro teachers equal pay, and led to desegregation of a number of graduate and professional schools. The prestige of the National Urban League declined among Negroes because it was reluctant to give aid to Negro labor unionists and because at that time its policies were widely believed to be influenced too much by white real estate interests. Consequently, the NAACP became the leader among Negro protest and betterment organizations. Although few Negroes participated directly in the formation and execution of its policies, the Negro populace closed ranks around it and agreed that its program offered the greatest hope for advancement.

For several years, the NAACP national leadership was almost exempt from criticism except from such avowed enemies as white supremacists and black nationalists. In the late 1950s, however, other organizations challenged the leadership of the NAACP, and many prominent Negroes questioned the wisdom of its goals and the efficacy of its techniques. Executive Secretary Roy Wilkins and the organization were subjected to a spate of criticism from other integrationists. Negro journalist Louis E. Lomax, himself a critic of the NAACP, attributes the growth of criticism to accumulating impatience with the NAACP, especially among young Negroes (Lomax, chap. 9). They object to its heavy reliance on the legal approach, and, more specifically, to its concentration upon school desegregation. The NAACP combats all types of discrimination, but for the last two decades or so, its primary goal has been to abolish segregated schools. Important as school desegregation is to future generations, today's adult Negroes are not directly benefited by it, nor are the 89 percent of Southern and Border Negro pupils who are still in all-Negro classes. The token desegregation of a previously all-white school may be a moral victory for all Negroes and may enhance their sense of worth, but the only immediate, tangible benefits are to the two or three Negro children involved. The fruits of victory often seem small in relation to the costs incurred, and some Negroes are left with a feeling that the effort was not worthwhile.

According to Lomax, the outburst of direct action—sit-ins, freedom rides, and other demonstrations—in the early 1960s was a revolt against the NAACP and the traditional Negro leadership as well as a revolt against whites. The increase in direct action grew out of impatience with the apparently slow and remote results of legal action: the techniques of the NAACP were not delivering enough benefits to enough Negroes at enough speed. But Lomax apparently overestimated the extent and persistence of Negro disenchantment with the NAACP. Ninety-one percent of the Negroes questioned by the Harris poll in a 1963 survey approved of the NAACP, whereas only 59 percent approved of the Congress of Racial Equality (CORE), the leading direct-action organization (*Newsweek*, July 29, 1963, p. 30). A study of Negroes in a Southern city revealed much more confidence in the effectiveness of the NAACP than in CORE (Killian and Grigg *a*, pp. 385–387). The NAACP national office is now giving greater support to direct action and may regain its prestige among direct-action advocates.

Although the Negro "revolt" of the 1960s was in part a criticism of the NAACP, it was the NAACP that was in large measure responsible for the yearnings and aspirations that prompted it. Had it not been for the earlier efforts of the NAACP, the court rulings it helped to bring about, and the great publicity given them, the Negro drive for equality would not have been so intense, and there would have been less frustration and impatience with the slow results of legal action. True, the direct-action organizations that rose to prominence during the revolt—CORE, the Student Nonviolent Coordinating Committee (known as SNCC), and Dr. Martin Luther King's Southern Christian Leadership Conference (SCLC)—momentarily stole the limelight from the NAACP, and the Association may never be the preeminent organization that it once was. Nevertheless, this much maligned, yet widely respected organization can claim a large share of the responsibility for the Negro "revolt" and the social changes the revolt precipitated.

The Shift to Direct Action

Only recently have many Negroes been willing to participate in open demonstrations, picketing, and boycotts. Heretofore, penalties against direct action would have been insupportably severe in the South; in the North, the great majority of Negroes gave little thought to such strategies or doubted their efficacy. In the rare instances when direct action was used, it generally failed to achieve its aims. The notable exception was the threatened march on Washington in 1941 that led to the issuance of Executive Order 8802 and the formation of the wartime Fair Employment Practices Committee. This exception presaged the recent successful strategies of direct action, the focusing of pressure on the federal government, and broad appeals to the whole nation.

MONTGOMERY BUS BOYCOTT

Thursday, December 1, 1955, marks the beginning of the era of direct action. On that day Mrs. Rosa Parks of Montgomery, Alabama, a middle-class Negro and former official in the local NAACP, was asked by a city bus driver to give up her seat to a white man. She refused and as a consequence was arrested. Word of the arrest spread, and within a few hours an *ad hoc* committee of middle-class Negro women was formed and called upon the Negro community to boycott the municipal buses (King, chap. 3). The next day a meeting of Negro leaders agreed that a boycott was in order. A young minister, the new pastor of middle-class Dexter Avenue Baptist Church, accepted the task of communicating the boycott decision to the 50,000 Negroes whose cooperation was essential if the plan was to succeed. Thus, the career as a race leader of Dr. Martin Luther King, Jr., was launched.

Most Negroes in Montgomery rallied to the leadership. Four days after Mrs. Parks' arrest, buses in the Negro section were without passengers—the bus company had lost an estimated 75 percent of its patronage. At a mass meeting that night, the Montgomery Improvement Association was formed to direct the boycott, and Dr. King was elected president. The association laid down the demands to be met before the boycott would be ended: (1) Negroes were to be guaranteed courteous treatment by bus drivers; (2) Negroes were to continue to sit at the back of the bus, but only if seats were allocated on a first-come-first-seated basis to Negroes and whites; and (3) Negro drivers were to be hired on routes that served predominantly Negro sections.

White reaction to the boycott was bitter, and the white leadership adamantly resisted the demands. Unsuccessful attempts were made to break the boycott—for instance, Dr. King was arrested on various charges and appeals were made to Negroes to depose him from leadership. They were told that no action would be taken on their complaints until they returned to the buses. But the Negroes persisted. They showed solidarity and determination unprecedented among Southern Negroes and continued to accept hardship and inconvenience rather than yield to white pressure. The movement had originated with middle-class Negroes, but it received mass support, without which it would have quickly collapsed. Participation was so nearly complete that white sanctions against individuals were ineffective. Negroes found that if they acted in unison, they could protest without losing their jobs. There were acts of terrorism and violence, but the Negroes endured them, sustained by the fearless example of Dr. King and the knowledge that each one shared his own danger and inconvenience with all others. The NAACP, which at first did not support the boycott, provided legal counsel when the Montgomery case came before the Federal District Court six months later. The court ruled against Montgomery's bus segregation ordinance, a ruling subsequently upheld by the Supreme Court, and the buses were completely desegregated—a victory beyond the original demands of the Montgomery Improvement Association. Direct action combined with legal action had won.

It is not easy to explain why Mrs. Parks refused to move from her bus seat that day in 1955, after decades of Negro acquiescence to similar and worse indignities. Nor is it easy to explain why the Montgomery Negro community acted with such unanimity when previously most Negroes stood by while "foolhardy" individuals suffered the consequences of breaches of race etiquette. Dr. King explains Mrs. Parks' action simply by saying that she "was a victim of both the forces of history and the forces of destiny. She had been tracked down by the *Zeitgeist*—the spirit of the time" (King, p. 35). The actions of Mrs. Parks and of the Montgomery Negroes were both expressions of social change and instruments of further change. The drift toward egalitarian values, the legitimacy given to Negro aspirations by the Supreme Court, the egalitarian and integration rhetoric that filled the mass media of communication—these, combined with accumulated resentment, replaced endurance with action. Negroes were aware that they were getting increased support in high places. Their accustomed resignation was being replaced with hope and the feeling that their condition could be changed.

Undoubtedly, there were many earlier individual acts in Southern cities that had been rebuffed and some acts that had succeeded but had not been given publicity. The Montgomery case is important because it became a contest between Negroes and segregationists, because it mobilized the Negro community, because it brought new leadership to the fore, because it gained national attention, and because Negroes gained their objective, albeit at some cost, after a prolonged effort. The issue was sufficiently clear and the necessary task sufficiently simple for tenacity, courage, and consensus to bring about success. A more complicated issue, requiring a shifting strategy, would have presented more difficulties in sustaining leadership and organizational effectiveness.

During the next few years, direct action spread throughout the South, inspired by Martin Luther King and often given support and direction by his SCLC. Urban middle-class ministers, who for the most part had functioned as accommodating leaders, followed his example and began to lead efforts to end segregation. The relative prosperity of their congregations reduced their dependence upon whites and freed them to take action. Dr. King became the most popular Negro in the country (Lomax, p. 96). His doctrine of nonviolence and his reliance on passive resistance had a strong appeal to Southern Negroes, whose religion taught that it is sinful to hate and that they should love their oppressors (Vander Zanden *b*, p. 547). Dr. King formulated a philosophy that reconciled the protest motive with Christian doctrine; he redefined protest activity as an expression of love rather than hate and consequently helped remove religious restraints from the urge to fight discrimination.

THE GREENSBORO SIT-IN

In spite of its spread in the South, direct action did not become the characteristic form of Negro protest until the 1960s. The next major event after the bus boycott that gave impetus to direct action occurred early in 1960 in Greensboro, North Carolina. Like the refusal of Rosa Parks to give up her seat and the subsequent boycott, this incident was a reaction of individual middle-class Negroes; it was not planned and instigated by any action organization. Four freshmen from the local Negro college sat down at a dime-store lunch counter, which until then served only whites, and refused to leave when they were denied service. The manager retaliated by closing the counter, whereupon the students opened their books and began to study. News of the demonstration soon reached the college, and dozens of other students poured into town and joined it.

A local adult Negro leader asked CORE to aid the students, and the organization sent field workers to conduct classes in nonviolent mass protest. Although twenty years old, CORE was a little known organization. It had long advocated mass direct action, and its fame was to grow as such action became prevalent. Dr. King and, somewhat later, the national office of the NAACP, also came to the aid of the movement, but CORE was the first on the scene and for some time the main supporter. Later, SNCC was organized to carry on student protest, and was financed largely by contributions from Northern college students and Dr. King's SCLC.

Sit-ins soon spread throughout the South and into some Northern and Western states. Although not universally successful, they brought about desegregation of a large number of lunch counters and similar service facilities. Such achievements may seem remote from the more basic educational and economic problems, but they made an important impact on Negro morale. Unlike token desegregation of schools, the effects were immediate and tangible and benefited Negroes of all ages and economic classes. Perhaps more important, thousands of Negroes had the satisfaction of participating directly rather than passively observing the small dramas in which NAACP lawyers, a few selected Negro pupils, and the white opposition were the only actors. Negroes could for the first time express their hostility against the traditional pattern of race relations with relative impunity; if they were penalized, they gained the satisfaction of suffering for a worthy cause.

BOYCOTTS

The most successful sit-ins were coupled with boycotts. The demonstrations were in themselves forms of economic pressure on the whites: they sometimes forced target establishments to close temporarily and they tended to keep white patrons away. However, lunch counters are usually only a minor source of profit for variety and department stores, and a Negro boycott of the entire establishment would greatly intensify the economic pressure. In Nashville, among other cities, the entire downtown business district was boycotted, and this brought pressure upon recalcitrant lunch counter operators from other businessmen.

As the sit-ins spread, the economic boycott was quietly developed as a separate form of pressure, not only to open public facilities but also to force employment and upgrading of Negroes. For instance, in 1960 some 400 Negro ministers in Philadelphia organized the "Selective Patronage Movement" and through a series of successful boycotts forced firms to hire more Negroes (Shaw). In the first year, the boycott was used against a dozen big companies—including Sun Oil, Gulf Oil, Tasty Baking, and Pepsi-Cola—and each yielded, Sun Oil after two and a half months but most of the others within a few days. About 600 Negroes were added to the payrolls of these companies, mainly in white-collar jobs. Through the cooperation of churches, lodges, and clubs, the boycott of Sun Oil products spread throughout Pennsylvania and sporadically up and down the East Coast from Boston to South Carolina. The word went out to Negro congregations: "Until the Pastor says so, not a drop of Blue Sunoco." And they obeyed.

Negro boycotts have not been so successful in many other cities. For a boycott to succeed, Negroes must account for a significant proportion of the sales of target firms. In Philadelphia, Negroes comprise more than 25 percent of the population, have perhaps more than 15 percent of the purchasing power, and probably account for 25 percent of the sales of soft drinks and some other products. Firms dealing in luxury goods, however, which would be little affected by a Negro boycott, have not been targets of the Philadelphia movement. A second requirement is that white feeling against the Negro action must not be so strong that white counterboycotts will be organized. (In the Deep South, notably in Birmingham, Alabama, such white countermeasures have been planned but so far not carried out.) Even in the North, boycotts must be conducted so as to minimize white resistance, since white counterboycotts and, in some states, legal measures could upset the Negro action. Perhaps fortunately for the Negro cause, the Philadelphia program has not been highly publicized. Although the subject of articles in the *Wall Street Journal* and *U. S. News and World Report,* it has been given little coverage in the local press and many white Philadelphians are not aware of it. No white person has lost his job because of the boycotts, and although a few whites may not have been hired because some jobs were given to Negroes, they probably are unaware of the reason.

A boycott may succeed even when the Negro population is relatively small. For instance, in the spring of 1961 picketing and a loosely organized boycott in Champaign-Urbana, Illinois, opened sales and clerical jobs to Negroes even though the 6,500 Negroes in the community were only about 8 percent of the total population and probably had no more than 5 or 6 percent of the purchasing power (Bindman *b*, chap. 1). The community was unusual, however, in that a large number of whites supported the Negro action. A sizable proportion of the 2,500 faculty families and 25,000 students at the main campus of the University of Illinois—a larger and more affluent segment of the community than the Negroes— joined the boycott. The action was also aided by the fact that its main target, a new J. C. Penny store, catered to low- and medium-income clientele, among whom Negroes were relatively numerous. A few whites in many other communities, including even Nashville, have joined Negro boycotts, but white participation is not usually decisive, as it probably was in Champaign-Urbana.

Under some conditions, the economic boycott is one of the strongest pressure techniques available for influencing employment practices. It places employers in a position where their self-interested action benefits Negroes. Boycotts may become more frequent, but so far they are not so popular as demonstrations, perhaps because participation in a boycott involves less overtly expressive behavior and less direct release of hostility and tension. Furthermore, direct and immediate benefits accrue only to a few people, and some Negroes are reluctant to undergo the inconvenience of a boycott so that others can advance. Low-status Negroes, who lack qualifications for the new jobs and whose racial identification tends to be weak, are often reluctant to participate. On the other hand, the Champaign-Urbana boycott was started and strongly supported by Negroes who, having high status, did not themselves benefit from the opening of sales and clerical jobs. To these Negroes, the refusal of firms to hire Negroes for white-collar work was an insult, and their racial identification was strong enough for racial gains to be experienced as personal gains. To an increasing extent, however, race pride, hope for better opportunities for children and grandchildren, and the influence of ministers and other leaders draw into boycotts and other race activities even the very poor and poorly educated, though they remain the least enthusiastic participants.

THE FREEDOM RIDES

Not much more than a year after the beginning of the sit-ins, another major form of protest, the "freedom rides," was initiated by James Farmer, former program director of the NAACP and the new director of CORE. The rides—long trips on chartered buses—were designed to test racial discrimination at interstate travel terminals. Although the Supreme Court had ruled in 1958 that terminal segregation violated the Interstate Commerce Act, almost all bus terminals in the South kept segregated facilities. The first ride, made in the spring of 1961 by Farmer, six other Negroes, and six whites on a route from Washington, D. C., to New Orleans, was followed by about a dozen others, participated in by more than a thousand persons, and sponsored by all four major Negro action organizations. White Southerners responded to the freedom rides more violently than they had to the sit-ins. At bus terminals, riders were repeatedly met by hostile whites, and the local law-enforcement officials often failed to give the riders adequate protection. Many riders were beaten and on one occasion a bus was burned. Although the riders were often refused service or found all terminal facilities closed, in the long run they attained their objective. The Interstate Commerce Commission issued an order banning segregation in interstate terminal facilities, and Southern compliance was soon widespread, although not universal.

An equally important consequence was that the freedom rides stimulated other direct action. James Farmer became one of the top Negro leaders and the membership of CORE grew rapidly. Demonstrations increased in number and variety through 1962, and the wave of activity in 1963 made all previous protest seem but a ripple in comparison. Scarcely a city in the nation escaped some kind of demonstration, the objects of protest ranging from segregation in public facilities to *de facto* school segregation, from discrimination in labor unions to segregation in churches. There were sit-ins, kneel-ins, wade-ins, and a massive, orderly, and well-organized "March on Washington" in August of 1963 that involved perhaps 200,000 people, both Negroes and whites. From press accounts, it is hard to determine whether there was more activity in the North or in the South. Demonstrations erupted even in the previously tranquil West and in small towns in the Mountain states with only a few Negro residents.

PASSIVE RESISTANCE

From the Montgomery action in 1955 through the widespread protests of 1963, the most prevalent type of protest was passive resistance. As developed by Mahatma Gandhi, widely used in India and in South Africa, and popularized among Negro Americans by Martin Luther King, passive resistance is a method by which dissatisfied elements of a society try to effect social change by nonviolent, nonrevolutionary means. Specific laws are the objects of attack, but the legal system itself is not attacked. On the contrary, legal process is deliberately used to elicit support and sympathy. Participants quietly accept arrest, refuse to pay bail, and choose imprisonment rather than pay fines. Defiant acts are carefully planned so as to minimize resentment from sympathetic or neutral elements in the dominant population (Kuper, esp. pp. 42–43).

To succeed in its objectives and to dramatize aspirations by nonviolent acts, a passive resistance movement must have a sophisticated leadership, capable of planned action. The rank and file must be disciplined and restrained from impetuous or opportunistic behavior that would subvert the idealism of the movement and compromise its aspirations. Most important, the movement must defend itself from being taken over by exponents of violence, either organized activists or uncontrolled mobs.

As we point out above, this nonviolent type of protest has

appeal for Negro Americans because it is acceptable to the conscience of people imbued with the Christian taboo against violence and hate. Perhaps more important, passive resistance is one of the most effective methods of protest available. Negroes have limited access to funds and the most powerful individuals in the local community; they simply do not have the resources to pursue their aims by means of violent coercion, and only a few extremists espouse violence. On the other hand, Negro Americans and other low-income, poorly educated minorities have a source of strength because of the division of labor and social interdependence. Their cooperation is essential for the performance of vital service functions, and they can exert pressure merely by refusing to cooperate (Vander Zanden *b, p.* 544). Negroes have long expressed hostility and resisted white control through noncooperation: by not showing up for work or not "understanding" orders or "accidentally" breaking equipment. But these are "wildcat" individual tactics. In the passive resistance movement, noncooperation is collective, planned, and organized.

In response to organized noncooperation, whites try to coerce Negroes, but coercion becomes progressively more difficult. Passive resistance tends to be cumulative, flooding the jails and courts with violators so that law-enforcement facilities are strained to the breaking point. An element of irony runs through the protest behavior: The full police power of a municipality can be engaged to enforce an ordinance that regulates who may sit at a dime store lunch counter. But irony is lost in the urgency of the moment and in the larger significance of events.

MASS PROTEST

Large-scale passive resistance is first of all a way to mobilize the minority population and dramatize discontent. It is designed to embarrass whole communities and even the nation into concessions and support. Usually such actions are not directed at a single grievance, although they may be precipitated by a minor incident. Rather they are general protests, calling for redress in the broadest terms and pointing to historical error and moral wrong as justification for action. Such resistance is complex in origin, in form, and in implications. It plays upon fear as well as idealism. It is a show of strength even though the participants may lie limp in the streets waiting for the police. Leaders like James Farmer of CORE and A. Philip Randolph insist that they intend demonstrations to be nonviolent, orderly, and disciplined. To a remarkable degree, these standards have been achieved—for example, in the 1963 March on Washington. The march was an unusual rally in that it was planned long in advance and well publicized, carried out in the light of day and in the eyes of the world. It was religious in its tone, it released rather than generated tensions of active participants, and it aroused the sympathy of passive viewers.

The Negro protest movement to a great extent has been true to the ideal of nonviolence. Instances of demonstrators initiating violence or responding in kind are few. In no case do the leaders of the large protest organizations condone violence—they are aware that it could have critical repercussions on their long-term objectives—but they do accept risks. Large numbers of people, particularly those untrained in the objectives of a movement and undisciplined in their conduct, may get out of control. A style of protest that had gained a degree of public acceptance may be submerged in unacceptable actions, resulting in damage to a whole movement and discredit to the sponsoring organizations.

Apparently, the hazards are greatest when protest rallies are held in segregated areas within a city. A rally is intended to mobilize energies and emotions, but if a constructive task is not at hand, tensions are built up without release, and there is a serious risk of loss of control. A sit-in or a boycott has a clear objective, and discipline can usually be maintained even over a long period and despite serious provocation. But a protest rally such as that held in Harlem in July 1964, against alleged police brutality, has no clear task that can be accomplished; and it is not in itself a complete drama as was the 1963 March on Washington. Even if it is not used as a cloak for looting and rioting by criminal and delinquent elements, such a demonstration entails an extraordinary risk. Leaders of protest organizations are learning from bitter experience how to estimate the hazards of holding rallies during periods of tension and where the rallies may be held most safely. At the same time, extremists are learning how to foment disorder, and criminals under the cover of public disturbance are becoming bolder in attacks on the police and property.

Other departures from the first principles of passive resistance, as set forth by Mahatma Gandhi, Dr. King, and others, have been fairly numerous. Inevitably, as the number of demonstrations increased, there was a decline on the average in the care taken in their planning, in the responsibility of their leadership, and in their effectiveness. Local Negro leaders, often unsophisticated and unschooled in techniques of mass protest, made numerous tactical errors: demonstrations were poorly timed and targets poorly selected. Often the activity resulted in only a minimal amount of effective pressure or antagonized influential whites whose cooperation was needed. Protest activity tended to become more expressive and less instrumental. Demonstrations became less focused upon those primarily responsible for discrimination. For instance, the Brooklyn chapter of CORE, in opposition to the national office, planned a "stall-in" at the opening of the New York World's Fair in the spring of 1964. Negroes were to drive their cars onto the expressways leading to the fair, deliberately run out of gas, and thus block traffic. Another plan proposed that Negroes leave their faucets on, thus wasting millions of gallons of water. Neither plan was executed, partly because of strong opposition from responsible Negro leaders who opposed the harassment on principle and who correctly perceived that even those whites sympathetic to the Negro cause would give priority to public welfare and safety and would oppose the actions, thus perhaps permanently handicapping the struggle for Negro rights.

In other cases, the protests, though well focused upon discriminators or alleged discriminators, used techniques that went beyond what most liberal whites and many Negro leaders considered justifiable. For instance, in 1964 in the San Francisco Bay area, Negroes entered supermarkets whose employment practices they considered to be discriminatory, loaded baskets with groceries, wheeled them to the check-out counters in the front of the stores, and then walked out, leaving the store employees to return the items to the shelves. The detrimental effects on the stores were less than those of a well-organized boycott, but many persons who would have supported a boycott considered the technique to be unwarranted harassment. However, the choice of such a technique is understandable. It more effectively expressed hostility than a boycott, it was easier to execute, and it required the cooperation of fewer people.

Although they oppose the more extreme measures, most Negro leaders believe that on the whole such demonstrations have aided Negro advancement. According to one rationale, they awaken the conscience of whites and arouse their guilt feelings. It is believed that most whites tend to repress their guilt by avoiding awareness of discrimination and the plight of Negroes. The demonstrations supposedly make such repression and avoidance more difficult. It is also believed that demonstrations keep politicians and public officials aware of Negro demands and increase the likelihood of favorable legislation and rulings by courts and regulatory agencies.

The validity of these assumptions is open to question. The earlier direct action was apparently quite effective, but it was the accompanying economic pressure and legal force that were the most potent influences for change. The effectiveness of demonstrations that do not exert economic pressure or that do not force the testing of legislation or the implementation of court rulings is often negligible. The belief that Negro direct action activates the white conscience is especially in doubt. True, the feelings of many whites who strongly favor Negro rights have been intensified by the events of the last two or three years, but so have the feelings of whites who strongly oppose Negro demands. Careful research has not established the effects upon the attitudes of whites between the two extremes, but it is our impression that demonstrations have aroused fear and resentment as often as guilt.

Perhaps fear, resentment, *and* guilt are aroused simultaneously, but whatever the emotions, it is not inevitable that they will be expressed in a manner favorable to the Negro cause.

Public opinion polls indicate that demonstrations have not gained white support. Only 21 percent of the whites surveyed by a 1963 Gallup poll said they believed that demonstrations help the Negro cause, and a year later the figure fell to 10 percent (American Institute of Public Opinion press release, June 15, 1964). Perhaps most whites felt that demonstrations had not helped the Negro cause because they had not themselves become more sympathetic. This view is supported by a 1963 Harris poll, in which a majority of whites said they thought Negroes were moving too fast and that most kinds of demonstrations were not justified (*Newsweek,* October 21, 1963, pp. 44–45). However, it does not necessarily follow that many of these whites will actively oppose Negro demands or that active supporters of the Negro cause have been alienated.

There is evidence, however, of a white "backlash," as the press has called it, to the so-called Negro revolt. For instance, in the spring of 1964, one of the strongest segregationists, Governor George Wallace of Alabama, entered Democratic primaries as a Presidential candidate in Wisconsin, Indiana, and Maryland. In each case, he opposed a candidate pledged to support President Lyndon Johnson, and in each state he received a substantial percentage of the Democratic vote: 34 percent in Wisconsin, 30 percent in Indiana, and 43 percent in Maryland, where the white vote was almost evenly divided between Wallace and Senator Brewster. Although Wallace denied that race was an issue in his campaigns, emphasizing instead "states rights" and a general opposition to extension of federal controls, race was the basic issue for many who voted for him. In Maryland, his heaviest support came from localities where the Negro population was relatively large and where there had been numerous demonstrations. In all three states, he drew heavy support from working-class (mostly ethnic) neighborhoods near expanding Negro districts and from many, although not all, middle-class all-white suburbs. Working-class people of recent immigrant stock are not predominantly conservative, and therefore their votes for Wallace were clearly a reaction to a perceived threat from Negroes. The suburban vote for Wallace may reflect a more general conservatism and opposition to the extension of federal controls, but many suburbanites were probably fearful of having Negro neighbors and resentful of Negro demands that would upset the neighborhood basis of schools. However, in the Presidential election in the fall of 1964, the "backlash" seemed to have little effect outside of the South, other issues apparently having outweighed the civil rights issue.

The fact that white resistance to Negro demands has stiffened, at least to the extent that for the first time anti-Negro or anti-civil rights sentiments are affecting the voting of many whites outside the South, does not in itself mean that Negro strategy has been defective. Everything else being equal, the less white resistance there is, the more rapidly Negroes can advance, but minimizing white resistance is not the primary goal of Negro leadership. Any pressure for change that threatens vested interests, as Negro protest does, is bound to elicit stiff resistance; and the price of minimal resistance—little or no open agitation—may be more than Negroes care to pay. However, from the standpoint of achieving goals, action that unnecessarily evokes white resentment and fear is detrimental, and some Negro demonstrations have done this. On the other hand, many expressive demonstrations, even though they do not effect any objective gains, fill a psychological need. The increased preoccupation of Negroes with discrimination and the wrongs they have suffered, a necessary part of the Negro awakening, has increased Negro hostility and resentment, or at least has tended to focus existing hostility on whites. This hostility almost certainly will be expressed in one way or another, and nonviolent protest is the outlet least detrimental to the Negro cause. Furthermore, demonstrations strengthen Negro solidarity and *esprit* and therefore they increase capacity for other kinds of concerted action. Participation in protest activity, irrespective of the ultimate objective, tends to transform the Negro individual (Pettigrew *b*, p. 167). He tends to grow in self-esteem, assertiveness, and readiness to assume an active role as a citizen.

Negro leaders have grown more sensitive to the fact that under some circumstances demonstrations do more harm than good and are trying to discourage such activity. For instance, Roy Wilkins, executive secretary of the NAACP, urged Negroes to use prudence and discretion in demonstrations for white compliance with the Civil Rights Act of 1964. Confidence of the Negro populace in the efficacy of demonstrations has also declined. Seventy-two percent of the Negroes questioned in a Gallup poll in 1963 said they believed that demonstrations help the Negro cause, compared with only 55 percent a year later (American Institute of Public Opinion press release, June 15, 1964). In June 1964, however, only 22 percent believed that demonstrations hurt, and 23 percent were undecided or thought that they made no difference. But this was before the rioting of the summer. It seems likely that the violence of the summer months discredited demonstrations, but such a change in opinion may have little effect upon their incidence. Those whose views shifted may have been nonparticipants. The change in opinion may, but probably does not, signal a shift away from direct action.

5

Education

Negroes in the United States have been called an under-developed nation in need of emergency aid. Although the figure of speech is plausible in some ways, it is far-fetched in others. The emergency is real, but Negroes do not need training in agriculture nor in manual skills nor do many Negro youth need training for rudimentary literacy. In comparison with the populations of underdeveloped countries, Negro Americans are highly skilled and well educated. If American economy and technology were not changing so rapidly, requiring more expertness, more education, and higher skills, a moderate effort over a few decades would modernize the Negro labor force. The educational difficulties of Negroes are compounded by technological change, by the fact that white youth is seeking more education, and by rising educational standards that put pressure on all youth. And Negro youth is burdened by a long history of educational deprivation, and, for the majority, by a home background with few books and little awareness of the nature and value of formal education.

In a highly industrialized nation, education is the key to the job and increasingly the measure of the man. Education says what a man can do, and it is the best single predictor of what he will do. Where does the Negro stand? How did he get there? What are the prospects for improvement of his educational status? Will he soon be able to catch up with whites?

Although Negroes are still far behind whites in amount of formal education, their educational status—in absolute terms and compared with that of whites—has almost continuously improved since emancipation. At that time, few Negroes had formal schooling, and more than four-fifths were illiterate. In the decades after the Civil War, Negro illiteracy declined steeply (see Fig. 1), but not until 1900 did it fall below 50 percent and not until 1920 did it fall below 25 percent. In 1960, less than one in ten Negroes was illiterate—a remarkable improvement—but in 1960 Negroes had only caught up to the literacy level of whites in 1890. Today, less than one white in fifty is illiterate.

In 1860, only 2 percent of Negroes of school age were attending school. The proportion jumped from a tenth in 1870 to a third in 1880, leveled off for the next two decades, and then increased in an unbroken trend. The change from 1890

TABLE 1. PERCENTAGE OF PERSONS 5 THROUGH 20 YEARS OLD ATTENDING SCHOOL, BY RACE, UNITED STATES, 1890–1960

Year	Negro	White	Ratio of Negro to white
1890	32.9	57.8	.57
1900	31.0	53.6	.58
1910	44.7	61.3	.73
1920	53.5	65.7	.81
1930	60.0	71.5	.84
1940	64.4	71.8[a]	.90
1950	71.3[b]	75.7	.94
1960	78.7[b]	82.2	.96

SOURCE: *U.S. Census of Population: 1930*, II, p. 1094; *U.S. Census of Population: 1940*, II, Part I, p. 37; and *U.S. Census of Population: 1960*, Final Report PC (1) -1D, p. 372 (U.S. Bureau of the Census, Washington, D.C.) .

[a] Native whites only.

[b] Includes other nonwhite races.

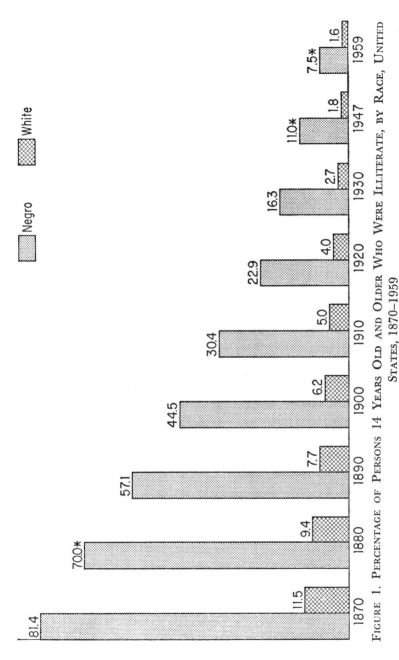

FIGURE 1. PERCENTAGE OF PERSONS 14 YEARS OLD AND OLDER WHO WERE ILLITERATE, BY RACE, UNITED STATES, 1870–1959

SOURCE: *U.S. Census of Population: 1930*, vol. II, p. 1223 and *Statistical Abstract of the United States, 1963*, p. 123 (U.S. Bureau of the Census, Washington, D.C.).
*Includes other nonwhite races.

through 1960 is shown in Table 1. As important as the absolute increase in Negro school attendance is the decrease in the difference between that of Negroes and whites. By 1960, the nonwhite percentage was only slightly below the white percentage and was actually above the white percentage of a decade earlier.*

Years in School

The median years of school completed by nonwhites 25 years old and older rose from 5.8 in 1940 to 6.9 in 1950 to 8.2 in 1960. The white median also rose appreciably, but the percentage increase was not so much; therefore, the ratio of the nonwhite to the white median went from .67 in 1940, to .71 in 1950, to .75 in 1960. The gap between white and nonwhite medians was greater for males than for females at each date, but the gap closed more for males. The ratio of nonwhite to white median years of school completed by males went from .62 in 1940, to .69 in 1950, to .74 in 1960. The female ratio went from .69 in 1940, to .72 in 1950, to .76 in 1960. If the 1940-to-1960 change in the ratios were extended, the nonwhite and white medians would be the same for males within 45 years from 1960, or by the year 2005, and would be the same for females about 72 years after 1960, or by the year 2032. These projections are not intended as predictions but are made only to show that at the recent rate of convergence, equality in median years of Negro and white education is still several decades away.

Indeed, equality in average educational attainment of adults is likely to come later than these projections indicate. Many people who are now young adults will live for many years, and their educational attainments will continue to affect the data. Complete educational equality will not be

---

* Many U.S. census reports do not distinguish Negroes from other nonwhites, and in a few places in this book the terms are perforce used interchangeably. Just before the admission of Alaska and Hawaii to statehood in 1959, about 95 percent of nonwhites in the United States were Negroes; in 1964 about 92 percent were Negroes.

attained for four or five decades after equality is attained in the young adult population. In 1960, there was a considerable educational gap between whites and Negroes 25 through 29 years old, most of whom had completed their formal education, but the gap was less than in higher age brackets (see Tables 2 and 3). The median years of school completed by nonwhite males was 10.5, or 85 percent of the 12.4 median years completed by white males. In the same age range, the nonwhite female median was 11.1 years, or 90 percent of the 12.3 white median. The gap both for males and females was greater at each higher age level and was much greater in the oldest age brackets—evidence of marked convergence. However, there must be parity at lower levels long before overall equality is attained.

In the urban population alone, young nonwhite adults were closer to educational equality, but in the rural farm population a big gap remained even at the youngest ages. (The gap in the rural nonfarm population, for which no data are given in Table 2, was intermediate between the urban gap and the rural farm gap.) Almost all rural Negroes are in the South, where discrimination is greatest and where the rural population in general is most disadvantaged. The educational facilities available to the rural Southern Negro are still poor; his isolated, economically and culturally deprived existence is not conducive to high educational aspiration or achievement. The few rural Negroes who become relatively well educated are likely to migrate to cities, where economic and occupational opportunities are better.

Consider the age group 25 through 29 in more detail. Although the difference in median years of school completed by nonwhite males (10.5) and white males (12.4) may seem small, it is important. It is important because the median white male was a high school graduate and the median nonwhite male was not. Median years do not reveal other important differences between the nonwhite and white educational distributions, some of which are shown in Table 3. Even though the gap between the medians was small, 64 percent of

TABLE 2. MEDIAN YEARS OF SCHOOL COMPLETED, BY AGE, COLOR, SEX,
AND PLACE OF RESIDENCE, UNITED STATES, 1960

	Male			Female		
Age	Non-white	White	Ratio of nonwhite to white	Non-white	White	Ratio of nonwhite to white
Urban and rural						
25–29	10.5	12.4	.85	11.1	12.3	.90
30–34	9.7	12.2	.80	10.5	12.3	.85
35–39	8.9	12.2	.73	9.7	12.2	.80
40–44	8.3	12.0	.69	8.7	12.1	.72
45–49	7.4	10.7	.69	8.1	11.2	.72
50–54	6.8	9.8	.69	7.6	10.4	.73
55–59	6.0	8.8	.68	6.9	9.2	.75
60–64	5.5	8.6	.64	6.4	8.8	.73
65–69	4.7	8.4	.56	5.6	8.6	.65
70–74	4.4	8.2	.54	5.2	8.5	.61
75 and over	3.9	8.1	.48	4.5	8.4	.54
Urban						
25–29	11.1	12.5	.89	11.5	12.4	.93
30–34	10.3	12.4	.83	10.9	12.3	.89
35–39	9.7	12.3	.79	10.2	12.3	.83
40–44	8.7	12.1	.72	9.1	12.2	.75
45–49	8.1	11.3	.72	8.5	11.6	.73
50–54	7.4	10.4	.71	8.1	10.7	.76
55–59	6.7	9.1	.74	7.4	9.6	.77
60–64	6.1	8.8	.69	6.8	8.9	.76
65–69	5.3	8.5	.62	6.1	8.6	.71
70–74	5.0	8.3	.60	5.7	8.5	.67
75 and over	4.4	8.2	.54	5.0	8.5	.59
Rural farm						
25–29	7.0	12.1	.58	8.3	12.2	.68
30–34	6.2	11.0	.56	7.8	12.1	.64
35–39	5.7	10.5	.54	7.2	12.0	.60
40–44	5.2	9.2	.57	6.9	10.9	.63
45–49	4.9	8.8	.56	6.5	10.1	.64
50–54	4.7	8.6	.55	6.3	9.2	.68
55–59	4.3	8.4	.51	5.8	8.8	.66
60–64	4.1	8.3	.49	5.4	8.6	.63
65–69	3.8	8.2	.46	4.7	8.4	.56
70–74	3.7	8.1	.46	4.5	8.3	.54
75 and over	3.3	7.8	.42	3.8	8.2	.46

SOURCE: *U.S. Census of Population: 1960*, Final Report PC (1)-1D, Table 173 (U.S. Bureau of the Census, Washington, D.C.) .

TABLE 3. PERCENTAGES OF PERSONS AT HIGHEST AND LOWEST EDUCA-
TIONAL LEVELS, BY AGE, COLOR, AND SEX, UNITED STATES, 1960

	Male			Female		
Age	*Non-white*	*White*	*Ratio of nonwhite to white*	*Non-white*	*White*	*Ratio of nonwhite to white*
Completed four or more years of college						
25–29	5.3	15.6	.34	5.4	8.1	.67
30–34	5.5	15.8	.35	4.8	7.6	.63
35–39	4.5	14.0	.32	4.2	6.5	.65
40–44	3.6	10.7	.34	3.7	6.5	.57
45–49	2.9	9.2	.32	3.3	6.5	.51
50–54	2.4	8.8	.27	3.1	6.8	.46
55–59	1.9	7.5	.25	2.3	5.7	.40
60–64	1.9	6.0	.32	1.9	4.5	.42
65–69	1.5	5.1	.29	1.5	3.8	.39
70–74	1.6	4.5	.36	1.5	3.2	.47
75 and over	1.4	4.1	.34	1.1	2.9	.38
Completed one or more years of college						
25–29	13.5	29.2	.46	12.7	19.8	.64
30–34	11.9	27.0	.44	11.2	18.6	.60
35–39	9.9	24.6	.40	9.3	17.3	.54
40–44	8.0	20.6	.39	7.9	16.3	.48
45–49	6.1	18.0	.34	6.6	16.2	.41
50–54	5.4	17.1	.32	6.4	16.9	.38
55–59	4.4	14.7	.30	5.0	14.8	.34
60–64	4.1	12.6	.33	4.5	12.5	.36
65–69	3.4	10.8	.31	3.7	10.9	.34
70–74	3.5	9.6	.36	3.7	9.6	.39
75 and over	2.9	8.7	.33	2.8	8.5	.33
Completed not more than four years of elementary school						
25–29	9.6	2.6		5.1	1.8	
30–34	12.6	3.0		7.0	2.1	
35–39	16.1	3.4		10.1	2.4	
40–44	22.0	3.8		14.2	2.7	
45–49	28.4	4.7		18.5	3.4	
50–54	33.7	6.1		23.1	4.7	
55–59	40.7	8.5		30.0	7.1	
60–64	45.5	11.6		36.1	10.1	
65–69	53.9	17.1		44.3	14.0	
70–74	56.4	21.4		48.3	16.0	
75 and over	62.4	24.1		55.1	17.0	

SOURCE: *U.S. Census of Population: 1960,* Final Report PC (1) -1D, Table 174
(U.S. Bureau of the Census, Washington, D.C.) .

whites of both sexes had completed four years of high school but only 39 percent of the nonwhites had done so. The percentage of white males who had completed four or more years of college was almost three times the nonwhite percentage. Furthermore, nonwhite males do not seem to be gaining on whites at this highest educational level, since the ratio of the nonwhite to the white percentage was almost the same at all ages. By contrast, the percentage of nonwhite females with four or more years of college has increased at a faster rate than has the percentage of white females at that level, and in 1960 the nonwhite percentage was two-thirds of the white percentage at ages 25 through 29.

Dropouts

The differences between the percentages who completed four or more years of college and the percentages who completed one or more years of college provide estimates of college dropouts after the first year and before completion of college. (These estimates are somewhat low, since not all who finish four years of college actually complete the course of study and receive degrees.) Sixty-one percent of nonwhite males 25 through 29 years old in 1960 who had completed at least one year of college had not completed four years, compared with only 47 percent of comparable white males. A very small number of these males were still enrolled in college, but most had dropped out. In contrast to males, nonwhite females in the same age range showed about the same staying power as white females; the estimated dropout percentages were 57 and 59, respectively.

Several factors account for the high dropout rate of nonwhite males. The quality of Negro education below the college level is still inferior to white education in all regions of the country, and therefore many poorly prepared Negroes drop out because of academic failure. However, if poor preparation were the main reason for the high dropout rate of nonwhite males, one would expect a similar rate for nonwhite females. Furthermore, most Negro college students were enrolled in predominantly Negro institutions in which standards are not high and a poor background is less handicap. Lack of adequate financial resources, the need to take jobs to help support relatives, and other economic reasons are perhaps at least as important as academic failure in accounting for the high dropout rate of nonwhite males.

There has been a widespread belief among Negroes that if they completed college they could not find employment suitable to their qualifications, and this belief has discouraged development of the diligence and tenacity needed to earn a college degree. In fact, the belief is no longer valid in the case of Negroes in most specialties (see Chapter 6), but Negro college students of the early and middle 1950s were not fully aware of the opportunities that had opened and were soon to open to Negro college graduates. In contrast to males, well-educated Negro females traditionally faced less discrimination and were able to find employment more nearly commensurate with their education. Consequently, a college education was considered a better investment for a Negro woman than for a Negro man (Cuthbert, pp. 17–18). Unlike most white parents, many Negro parents were (and perhaps still are) more willing to make sacrifices to send a daughter to college than to send a son.

Although the percentage of nonwhites with four years or less of formal schooling has steadily declined (from 41.8 in 1940, to 32.6 in 1950, to 23.5 in 1960 in the 48 conterminous states*), about 10 percent of males and 5 percent of females 25 through 29 years old were at this low educational level in 1960. The percentage for males was three and a half times larger for nonwhites than for whites, and for females it was roughly three times larger. In middle-age categories, from a fifth to a third of nonwhite males had completed less than five years of school. The percentage of nonwhites with very little formal education has declined each successive genera-

* I.e., those having a common boundary: the United States excluding Hawaii and Alaska.

tion and may soon be very small among the youngest adults, but the percentage in the total adult population will necessarily be fairly large for several more decades. The importance of this fact is underscored by decreasing occupational opportunities for poorly educated persons and consequently by increasing frustration and restiveness in the lower levels of Negro society.

Quality of Education

The preceding paragraphs have emphasized the importance of quantitative differences in Negro and white education, as measured by differences in years of school completed. The differences in the end products of education are even greater because the knowledge and skills gained from a year of school by and large are less for the Negro. The worth of a year of school varies according to the native ability, background, and incentive of the individual and according to the quality of the instruction and the situation in which it is imparted. With the exception of native ability, which is believed to be about the same for both races, these factors are on the average weighted in favor of whites. Differences in student background and in quality of instruction make the average Negro year of school far from equivalent to the average white year. These differences exist to varying degrees in all parts of the country. Available data do not permit of precise measurement of the difference in quality of Negro and white education, but an examination of some of the relevant evidence is indicated.

Before desegregation of public schools began, the inferiority of Negro education in the Southern and Border states was conspicuously evident from differences in per-pupil expenditures, length of the school term, pupil-teacher ratios, formal education of teachers, teachers' salaries, and the like. (These differences are of more than historical and regional importance, since a large part of the Negro labor force throughout the country was educated in the Southern and Border states during these years.) For instance, in Mississippi in 1943-1944, the expenditure per pupil was $71.65 for whites and only $11.96 for Negroes (MacIver, pp. 37–38). By 1953-1954, the expenditures had risen to $98.15 and $43.17 respectively. Even in 1960-1961, the Mississippi per-pupil expenditures, beyond the state's minimum allotments, were $81.86 for whites and only $21.77 for Negroes (*Southern School News,* February 1962). Mississippi was the extreme case of inequality, but substantial differences in financial support of Negro and white schools at one time existed in all states that maintained separate Negro schools and in the District of Columbia. In 1952, in Alabama, Arkansas, Florida, Georgia, Mississippi, North Carolina, and South Carolina, considered together, the expenditure per Negro pupil in the public schools was 76 percent of the expenditure per white pupil in metropolitan districts and 62 percent in rural districts (Ashmore, p. 155). Earlier, the disparity was much greater: in 1929-1930, in these same seven states, the comparable figure for Negro pupils was only about 25 percent.

Growing pressure for desegregation of the schools during the late 1940s and early 1950s led Southern cities and counties to increase financial support to Negro schools in attempts to forestall desegregation. At the time of the 1954 school desegregation decision (*Brown v. Board of Education of Topeka*), expenditures per pupil were almost equal for Negroes and whites in several Southern and Border states, and in Oklahoma the expenditure for Negroes was slightly above that for whites. However, in no state was the support great enough to bring the quality of Negro physical plants and teachings staffs up to that of white schools. Much larger expenditures for Negro schools would have been necessary to make up for past neglect. After the school desegregation decision, there was a flurry of construction of Negro school buildings throughout the South—a part of the massive resistance to desegregation—and for a time capital expenditures for Negro schools were far greater than for white schools in many districts. White citizens in many Southern communities now point to the new, modern Negro school buildings and ask: "Why should the Negroes want to send their children to our school? Theirs is better."

The increase in financial support to Southern Negro schools no doubt improved the quality of instruction, but a modern building does not make a superior school. When the Supreme Court ruled in 1954 that "separate schools are inherently unequal," it based its ruling upon sound sociological and psychological principles. The Court was mainly concerned with damage to the personalities of children forced to attend separate schools. Separate schools are also unequal in academic effectiveness, regardless of relative financial support, partly because Negro and white teachers are not equally well qualified. Most Negro teachers in the South are graduates of poor and mediocre Negro colleges and therefore are on the average even less well qualified than white teachers trained in small church and state colleges in the South. Perhaps more important, a large majority of Southern Negro pupils have lower-class, culturally deprived family backgrounds, and in separate schools they associate mainly with other children from deprived backgrounds. It is well known that an important aspect of a child's learning experience in school is association with other children, yet in the Southern Negro schools ignorance reinforces ignorance and cultural deprivation reinforces cultural deprivation. These schools lack an intellectually stimulating atmosphere, and the Negro children who attend them are virtually denied firsthand contact with the mainstream of American culture and society.

The same factors depress the quality of education in the Negro ghettos of Northern and Western cities. Schools in urban Negro slums frequently have outdated and inferior physical facilities, are overcrowded, and have less qualified teachers (both Negro and white) than schools in "better" neighborhoods. In mixed Negro and white areas, where many schools are nonsegregated, conditions are often similar. If a majority of white pupils are from lower-class families, Negro pupils are still engulfed in a lower-class society. Some teachers in these schools, in a misguided expression of sympathy, "discriminate in reverse," that is, they give Negro pupils passing grades even when they do not do the work required of whites. The result is that although Negro schooling in the North and West is usually better than that in the South, it is still decidedly inferior to white schooling.

In view of the many factors that tend to depress the quality of Negro education, it is hardly surprising that Negro pupils at each grade level average lower than whites on scholastic achievement tests. The gap in achievement varies from locality to locality, but it apparently is appreciable in all regions. Since on the average, each year of school yields a smaller increment of knowledge and skills to the Negro pupil than it does to the white, the gap in achievement is greater at the higher grades. In some localities, Negro high school pupils on the average do only as well as whites three to four grades below them.

If he chooses a predominantly Negro institution of higher education, the Negro student continues to receive inferior formal schooling. And he is likely to choose a predominantly Negro college, even if he lives outside the Deep South, because his public schooling has left him ill-prepared to compete with whites. In 1960, there were approximately 106 predominantly Negro colleges and universities in the United States. Almost a third of these are unaccredited institutions that probably do not offer college-level work. About another third are accredited but mediocre. Less than a third compare favorably with even run-of-the-mill small state and private predominantly white colleges. A few Negro colleges and universities are good, although not superior—Howard University, in Washington, D.C.; Fisk University, in Nashville, Tennessee; the Atlanta University system; and perhaps two or three others. In 1960, predominantly Negro institutions of higher learning had a resident enrollment of 88,859, which included well over half of all Negro college students. A minority of them attended the few good colleges.

Many factors account for the generally poor quality of

Negro colleges. They have recruited a majority of their students from the inferior Negro public schools in the South, and this perforce has kept their standards low. They lack adequate financial support. For instance, in 1959, Negro colleges as a whole had an income of $1,171 per degree student, compared with $1,609 for other colleges (Doddy, p. 371). Physical facilities are relatively poor and faculties are the most poorly paid segment of academe. Poor salaries, heavy teaching loads, poor libraries and other facilities, and low prestige make it difficult for most Negro colleges to recruit competent faculty members. As the demand for college teachers becomes greater, the number of well-qualified professors available to Negro colleges becomes even smaller. These institutions must rely more and more upon Negro professors. With the shortage of trained personnel, even mediocre white professors can usually find better paying positions in more prestigeful colleges. And the number of well-qualified Negro professors is far from sufficient to staff the Negro colleges. According to a recent estimate, only about a hundred Negroes will receive Ph.D. degrees between 1963 and 1966 (Dean Leonard Beach of Vanderbilt University, quoted in *Southern School News,* January 1964), only one Ph.D. for each predominantly Negro college. Several of the more competent graduates will be employed by predominantly white colleges, government agencies, and private industry. Therefore, most new faculty members of Negro colleges will have no more than a master's degree, and all too often the colleges will resort to hiring their own graduates, as they have done in the past, thus perpetuating mediocrity.

The fact that most Negro colleges are in some way controlled by whites has not improved their quality. The president is usually a Negro, but he is accountable to a governing board that is white or predominantly white, or the college may be dependent upon white philanthropy. Consequently, the president may be called an "Uncle Tom," there may be less academic freedom than in small white colleges in the

South, and relations among the administration, faculty, and students typically are not harmonious.

We do not mean to imply that all graduates of predominantly Negro colleges are poorly qualified in their specialties. Even the poor colleges graduate a few individuals who, because of resourcefulness and high native ability, are able to surmount the handicap of inferior education and fare well in competition with whites and better educated Negroes. But these people could do even better if their college training had been better.

Just one of the many disadvantages of the predominantly Negro educational institution is that the students hear mainly their characteristic Negro dialect. The graduate of a Negro college is likely to mispronounce words and make grammatical errors. Regardless of how well qualified he may be in his specialty, his speech may handicap him when he seeks employment and social acceptance (Green, pp. 81–83).

A substantial proportion of all Negro college students are now enrolled in predominantly white institutions. Their college training on the average is superior to that of students enrolled in Negro colleges, but it is inferior to that of the majority of white college students. The predominantly white colleges in which most Negroes are enrolled are of relatively poor quality. Most colleges do not maintain records on the race of students, and it is therefore not possible to tell exactly where the Negro enrollment is, but the case of Illinois is instructive. In the fall of 1963, a census of Negro students at the main campus of the University of Illinois found fewer than 400 Negroes among approximately 26,000 students (Bindman *a*). Only about 3 percent of the Negroes attending college in the state were in residence on the main campus of the University, compared with about 15 percent of the whites. Other Illinois colleges and universities with high academic standards, such as the University of Chicago and Northwestern University, apparently enrolled even fewer Negroes than the University of Illinois. A large part of the

Negro students in the state, through choice or necessity, attended colleges with relatively low standards—not a surprising fact in view of their poorer preparation and backgrounds.

The above discussion on quality of Negro education makes evident that Negroes are not so close to whites in educational attainment as statistics on years of schooling might suggest. If closing the gap in quantity of education is not accompanied by a corresponding closing of the quality gap, true educational equality is even farther away than the projections earlier in this chapter indicate. The causes of the quality gap are perhaps even more unyielding than the causes of differences in number of years of school completed. An appreciable disparity in the average qualifications of Negroes and whites may remain long after near equality in amount of formal education is attained.

The difficulties faced by Negroes who wish to obtain a good education that will enable them to compete successfully with whites remain among the most stubborn obstacles to Negro advancement. Yet the future of Negro Americans depends, more than anything else, upon how rapidly and how completely these obstacles can be overcome. The prospects for speedy improvement are not good, in spite of the fact that the most highly publicized racial news during the 1950s was the desegregation of schools and colleges and the opening to Negroes of new educational opportunities.

School Desegregation

Desegregation of many schools in the Border areas and in the South has been important, but the effects on the quality of Negro education have not yet been as great as Negro leaders and white supporters had hoped. In the eleven former Confederate states, a very small percentage of Negro pupils attended classes with whites in the fall of 1964—about 2.1 percent, or about 84,000 in a total of nearly 3 million Negro pupils in the public schools (*Southern School News,* December 1964). There was no desegregation below the college

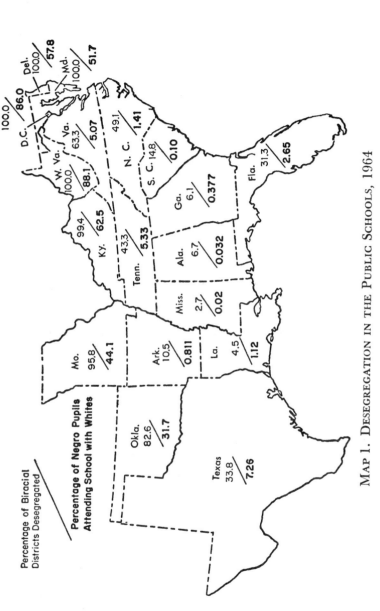

MAP 1. DESEGREGATION IN THE PUBLIC SCHOOLS, 1964

The numbers in this map are percentages. Above the diagonal is the percent of biracial districts that are desegregated in each state. Below the diagonal in dark numerals is the percent of Negro students actually attending schools with whites. SOURCE: *Southern School News* (Nashville: Southern Education Reporting Service, December 1964); after Broom and Selznick, p. 472.

level in Mississippi until 1964, and there and in Alabama and South Carolina only a minute fraction of 1 percent of all Negro pupils were in desegregated classes. Desegregation also directly affected less than 1 percent of the Negro pupils in Georgia and Arkansas. Desegregation was more widespread in Texas than in any other Southern state, but even there only about 25,000 Negro pupils (or about 7.3 percent) were enrolled in desegregated schools in 1964. The only appreciable effect of the desegregation decision upon the education of the nearly 3 million Negro school children in the South, ten years after the decision, was some improvement in the quality of Negro schools that resulted from white attempts to lessen pressure for desegregation. At the rate schools in the eleven Southern states were desegregated during the first decade after the decision, it would be more than *500 years* before all Negro pupils would be attending desegregated schools—a rate somewhat slower than "all deliberate speed." So far, in the Deep South the forces of segregation have held the line. However, about as much desegregation occurred in the South in 1964 as in the nine previous years combined, and if the rate continues to accelerate, an appreciable percentage of Southern Negro pupils may be attending school with whites within a few years.

The desegregation decision has had a more important effect in the Border areas. In Oklahoma, Missouri, and Kentucky a large majority of biracial districts were desegregated by 1964, and all biracial districts were desegregated in West Virginia, Maryland, Delaware, and the District of Columbia. However, in all of these states and in the District of Columbia, a substantial percentage of Negro pupils were enrolled in all-Negro schools, the consequence mainly of residential segregation, and, in some cases, of gerrymandering to create racially homogeneous school districts. In these six states and in the District of Columbia, 59.2 percent of the Negro pupils, or 315,471 of a total of 533,218 were enrolled in desegregated schools in 1964.

De facto racial segregation of schools, the result of residential segregation, remains prevalent in the North and West and may be increasing. In some cities, there is a continuing "resegregation": schools, once racially mixed, become all-Negro. Neighborhoods into which Negroes move are said to have a "tip point," that is, a percentage of Negroes beyond which remaining whites move out and the neighborhood becomes all-Negro. The "tipping" of neighborhoods often creates all-Negro schools. Schools also have a tip point. When the proportion of Negro pupils reaches that point, many parents of the remaining white children either move away from the district, even though they may live in an all-white area, or manage to transfer their children to other schools. Their action is not necessarily based on prejudice but often on the reasoning that if it is bad for Negro children to attend predominantly Negro schools, it is also bad for white children. This is the double-edged knife of the desegregation movement. Many Negro students are not desirable classmates for either whites or Negroes because they are poor students and because their manners and personal hygiene—exterior signs of a deprived background—are objectionable. Responsible and concerned parents, white and Negro, want to move their children from environments where learning is harder than it ought to be. White families can move more easily and do. Negro families that have a limited choice of places to live see the departure of white children from the school as a portent of declining educational opportunity. Unprejudiced white parents who move make the same decisions as prejudiced parents, and the disorderly changes in school enrollments go on.

Some Negro protest leaders have proposed that both Negro and white pupils be transported from their home neighborhoods to schools in other parts of the city to achieve racial balance. A few cities, including New York, do transport pupils, but the practice is not widespread. Strong objections have been raised to this proposed solution to *de facto* segregation, even by persons liberal on the race issue. Such transporting, it is claimed, disrupts the ties of the child to his neighborhood, ties that are often tenuous anyway, and helps create a rootlessness adverse to the emotional health of the child and to his proper socialization.

Another proposed solution is reverse gerrymandering, that is, redrawing district lines to restore racial balance. This kind of redistricting has been tried by a few cities. However, whites usually resist such a solution, and it is often not practicable. Negro neighborhoods in many cities expand so rapidly that frequent redistricting would be required to keep integration at the maximum, and such Negro ghettos as Harlem and the Chicago Black Belt are too big to be annexed in toto to adjacent white school districts. So the problem of *de facto* segregation persists.

Elimination of segregated schools has high priority in the contemporary Negro protest movement, and desegregation *is* necessary for attainment of educational equality. However, it is no panacea for the ills of Negro education. The short-run benefits of desegregation in the South and in Border states have not been great. For instance, the lowering of racial bars at colleges and universities in such Southern states as Florida and North Carolina has little meaning when so few Negroes have the necessary background and preparation to gain admission. In 1962, only about 7 percent of Negro high school seniors in Florida who took the Florida Twelfth Grade Test (an achievement test covering English, mathematics, science, social studies, and humanities) scored 200 or higher, the score required for unconditional admission into one of the state universities (Killian and Grigg *b,* p. 122). In contrast, 64 percent of white seniors who took the test scored 200 or above. For most Negro high school students, the lowering of racial bars came too late; they were too far behind to catch up. Killian and Grigg suggest that desegregation of the predominantly white state universities probably hurt the quality of education in the Negro colleges, where most Negro college students perforce must be enrolled, by draining off the few well-qualified Negro students (*op. cit.,* p. 123).

Some observers have suggested that entrance examinations

have been instituted at desegregated Southern colleges for the express purpose of limiting Negro enrollment. No manipulation of examination results would be needed for the examinations to serve this purpose, since few Negro applicants can pass an examination that most white applicants can pass. In fact, the tightening of entrance requirements is a nationwide response to nationwide problems: increased enrollment pressures resulting from the wartime "baby boom" and an increase in the proportion of young people going to college made some limitation on enrollment essential, if facilities were not to be overwhelmed. However, a consequence, intended or not, of instituting entrance examinations at such colleges as the Florida state universities and The University of Texas has been to keep Negro enrollments very small.

When Negro pupils are first placed in competition with whites in high school or in the upper elementary grades, they are usually too far behind to catch up. If standards are not lowered to accommodate the poorly prepared Negro students, more fail than would have failed in all-Negro schools. The stiffer competition may increase the emotional problems of Negro pupils, and they may become more likely to drop out. If there is a large proportion of poorly prepared students, the learning situation may be little better for any of the students than it would be in an all-Negro school. These are the penalties of desegregation that comes too late. The moral is clear enough. Extemporized strategies of school boards and courts too often invert the educationally correct desegregation process. If a step-by-step procedure is to be chosen, it will have most lasting effects if it is introduced from the bottom up. Nevertheless, most Negro pupils who enroll in previously all-white schools at any grade level gain more in the long run from their remaining schooling than they would have gained in all-Negro schools.

Desegregation at the lower grades brings greater benefits to Negroes (Simpson and Yinger, pp. 635–636), but even the Negro first grader may be too far behind his white classmates ever to catch up completely. His parents are likely to be semiliterate and to speak a lower-class dialect that will handicap the child in coping with the more nearly standard English he encounters in school. Rarely has he had the benefit of nursery school or kindergarten. Rarely has his home socialization prepared him for the discipline, routine, and competitiveness of the school. Consequently, he starts his formal education at a distinct disadvantage.

Any completely effective program for the equalization of Negro and white education, therefore, must include efforts toward equalization of preschool experiences. Complete equalization could be accomplished only by removing children from the family at a very early age—a "solution" not deserving serious consideration. However, a system of free nursery schools offering intensive training in spoken English and preparation for the school environment could begin early to overcome the cultural deficit of children from underprivileged homes. The long-range results of such a program would be well worth its cost. The children would get more from their later schooling, thus providing a greater yield from the public school tax dollar. And the presence of large numbers of Negroes in a class would no longer seriously impair the education of white pupils. The eventual savings in relief and welfare costs alone probably would pay for such a program. Under present conditions, school attendance for Negro children is often time-serving rather than learning. Compulsory school attendance laws are just that: they do not guarantee compulsory education.

Education and Discontent

Obtaining a good education remains difficult for Negroes, but the number of well-educated Negroes has increased markedly during recent decades. This increase has been a major factor underlying expressions of Negro discontent. Although the "Revolt of '63" spread to almost all segments of the Negro population, its primary impetus came from college students and young, college-educated Negroes. With improved education come higher aspirations and increased discontent with inferior social status. With improved education comes increased ability to express discontent and to organize effective protest activity. Those who oppose extending educational opportunities to subordinate populations correctly judge that education leads to unrest and troublesome ambitions. White Southerners during the post-Civil War period generally lacked enthusiasm for Negro education, except for manual training. They observed that uneducated Negroes were more willing to "stay in their place" and that educated ones were "uppity."

A recent study of the relationship between education and Negro discontent is instructive (Killian and Grigg *b,* pp. 37–43). About 600 Negroes in a Florida community were asked how satisfied they were with various aspects of their community and their situation in the community, including their jobs, job opportunities, educational facilities, public health and medical facilities, housing, and the like. From responses to all of these questions, a composite "community satisfaction score" was computed for each individual. A much larger percentage of high school graduates than of those with less education had very low satisfaction scores. However, a smaller percentage of Negro college graduates than of those who had completed only high school were very dissatisfied, partly because more college graduates had occupations appropriate to their education. Also, the community discontent of college-educated Negroes was probably somewhat mitigated by the satisfaction of being at the top of Negro society.

We point out in the next chapter that in the country as a whole, Negro males who had completed high school but had not completed college differed more in occupational status from their white educational counterparts than did Negroes at any other educational level. For this reason, if for no other, Negroes at this educational level have reason to be more dissatisfied than other Negroes. If they are, the recent increase in the proportion of adult Negroes in this education range (from about 11 percent in 1950 to about 18 percent in 1960) could account for much of the increase in Negro restiveness.

As the number of well-educated Negroes has increased, the discontent born of education has probably increased disproportionately. Well-educated Negroes are now numerous enough to reinforce one another's attitudes, and their "spirit of protest" has spread to many people with less education. One might guess that the growing number of well-educated Negroes finally reached a "critical mass" that resulted in an explosion of protest activity. However, such an explanation would be an oversimplification. Elsewhere we treat several other developments, some of which are associated with the increase in Negro educational status, that also contribute to the urgency of the drive for first-class citizenship.

6

Occupation and Income

During recent decades there have been improvements of the greatest consequences in the occupational and economic standing of Negro Americans. Viewed in absolute terms, these gains are impressive. For instance, in 1940 only 8.5 percent of employed Negro workers had white-collar or skilled manual occupations, whereas by 1960 almost 20 percent were employed in such work. The percentage employed as laborers and domestic service workers fell from 54 percent in 1940 to 33 percent in 1960. Unemployment in the non-white labor force fell during this period from 16.8 percent to 8.7 percent. The median wage and salary income of gainfully employed nonwhite males rose from $460 in 1939 to $3,023 in 1962. In actual buying power, in constant (1962) dollars, the increase was threefold—from $995 in 1939 to $3,023 in 1962.

However, these substantial occupational and income gains have not been sufficient to forestall Negro restiveness. Advancement may bring not satiation of ambition but desire for even greater advancement. Success is companion to a discovery of the possible and an increase in aspiration. But this is not the full story. Men evaluate their achievements not only in absolute but in relative terms, not only in dollars earned but also in relation to the earnings of co-workers and competitors. Many Negroes lack precise knowledge of the gap between Negro and white economic status, but they are nevertheless aware that the gap has not narrowed greatly. The satisfaction derived from increased prosperity has been diluted by the observation that whites are also more prosperous and that Negroes are nearly the same distance behind. Furthermore, the rate of Negro advancement, which was very rapid during World War II, declined during the postwar period and therefore fell far short of the hopes, kindled by wartime experience, that Negroes were at last catching up.

Improved occupational and educational status has made keener the Negro's perception of his relative disadvantage. For the first time, many Negroes have a vantage point from which to estimate with some accuracy their relative condition. A semiliterate agricultural laborer can easily tell that his economic status is far below that of most whites, but he is unlikely to be able to make a meaningful comparison. In contrast, an industrial worker knows where he stands in the labor hierarchy and can guess how far he would have to go to be on a par with white workers. A Negro college professor in a predominantly Negro college knows reasonably well what his degree is worth compared with the same degree (perhaps from the same institution) held by a white professor teaching in a neighboring university. Negroes now are not only more able but also more inclined to gauge their standing relative to whites because more of them have contacts with whites on an equal footing. Where Negro social isolation has decreased and egalitarian social contacts have increased, one effect undoubtedly has been a rise in aspirations and a heightened sense of deprivation. Because high income and high occupational status are rare among Negroes, the middle-status Negro (by white standards) ranks above most other Negroes and therefore enjoys high prestige in the Negro community (Glenn a). As long as he evaluates his economic status in relation to other Negroes, he may be fairly well satisfied, but when he begins to judge his status in relation to whites, he ranks himself lower and is less satisfied. To use the hackneyed metaphor, he is no longer a big frog in a little pond but a little frog in a big pond.

The Turning Point: World War II

Neither the occupational nor the economic gap between Negroes and whites was markedly closed between emancipation and the entry of the United States into World War II. In 1890, when the Census Bureau first gathered data on Negro occupations, almost 90 percent of Negro workers were in agriculture and domestic and personal service; about 60 percent of the native white workers were so employed. Early in the twentieth century, large numbers of Negroes moved from agriculture and domestic service into industrial occupations. However, there was an even greater movement of white workers, so that by 1940 only 20 percent of white workers remained in agriculture and domestic and personal service, compared with about 55 percent of Negro workers. In addition, many more white than Negro workers moved into skilled and white-collar occupations, resulting in a somewhat wider occupational gap between Negroes and whites in 1940 than in 1890. Accurate data on Negro and white incomes are not available for years prior to 1939, but there is little reason to believe that in 1939 Negro income compared more favorably with white income than it did late in the nineteenth century.

With the entry of the United States into World War II, Negro workers for the first time took a giant step toward equality with whites. The drafting of hundreds of thousands of civilian workers into the Armed Services created an acute labor shortage, and the dearth of qualified white males led to the recruitment of white women and Negroes of both sexes into types of work that previously had been largely closed to them. President Roosevelt's Executive Order 8802 in June 1941 forbade discrimination on the basis of race, creed, or national origin by employers who held government war contracts. The Fair Employment Practices Committee was set up to implement the order, and in several cases the committee was able to prevent discrimination and to open new jobs to Negroes. With the return of veterans to the civilian labor force at the end of the war, with the end of the Fair Employment Practices Committee in 1946, and with the decline of industries that mainly served the war effort, Negroes suffered losses in occupational status. However, not all wartime gains were lost, and conditions remained more favorable for Negro advancement than they had been before the war. Negro servicemen and workers in war industries gained valuable training and experience that enabled them to compete more effectively, and their employment in large numbers in unionized industries during the war left them in a stronger position in the labor movement. (Negroes first joined labor unions in large numbers after the founding of the CIO in 1935.)

However, the continuation of Negro gains after the war was not so much due to the residual effects of the war as to the nearly continuous prosperity and sustained growth of the whole economy. During and since the war, hundreds of thousands of new jobs have been created at intermediate and upper levels, and many Negroes have been able to move up without displacing whites (Glenn *d*, pp. 111–113). Between 1940 and 1960, the total number of employed white-collar workers increased by nearly 12 million, or 81 percent, while the total employed labor force increased by only 37 percent. Hundreds of thousands of white workers have moved into new higher-level jobs, leaving vacancies at intermediate levels that could be filled by Negroes. For instance, of white males 25 through 34 years old in 1950 who were employed as clerical and kindred workers, 61,000—or 9 percent—had moved out of these occupations or died by 1960 and had not been replaced by other white males of the same cohort (a "cohort" is made up of all persons born during a given period of time). Some of these whites were replaced by younger whites, but many were replaced by Negroes. Because Negro gains could occur without loss to whites, white resistance to Negro advancement was less than it otherwise would have been. Expansion of jobs at the upper levels is not a new trend; it goes back to the start of industrialization, but until recently the upward movement of workers generated by this change did not greatly benefit Negroes. As long as large numbers of European immigrants were entering the country, they, rather than Negroes, replaced most of the native-born whites who moved up. World War I slowed European immigration and the Immigration Act of 1924 reduced it to a mere trickle, so that by the 1940s there was no longer a large pool of immigrants at the lowest occupational levels to replace the upward-moving native workers. The opportunity for the first great occupational advancement of Negro Americans was at hand.

The Occupation Gap

Some aspects of the occupational advancement of employed Negroes in relation to employed whites from 1940 to 1960 are shown in Table 4. The "expected" proportion of Negroes in each occupational group is the proportion of Negroes in the total employed labor force. For instance, 8.4 percent of all employed males in 1960 were Negro, and one might "expect" 8.4 percent of employed males in each occupational group to be Negro. If the actual proportion of Negroes in an occupational group was more than this parity, the ratio is greater than 1.00; if the actual proportion was less than expected, the ratio is less than 1.00.

The greatest gains for both Negro males and females from 1940 to 1960 were in intermediate-level occupations, such as clerical workers, craftsmen, foremen, and operatives. There was negligible increase in the representation of Negro males in the highest-level occupations during the two decades. The ratio of the actual to expected proportion of employed Negro males who were managers, officials, and proprietors in-

TABLE 4. RATIO OF ACTUAL TO EXPECTED PROPORTION OF EMPLOYED
WORKERS WHO WERE NEGRO, IN EACH OCCUPATIONAL GROUP,
UNITED STATES, 1940, 1950, AND 1960[a]

	Male			Female		
Occupational group	1940	1950	1960	1940	1950	1960
Professional, technical, and kindred workers	.33	.29	.30	.33	.45	.55
Farmers and farm managers	1.44	1.28	.77	2.20	2.24	1.06
Managers, proprietors, and officials, except farm	.13	.19	.17	.19	.30	.28
Clerical and kindred workers	.19	.47	.70	.04	.14	.25
Sales workers	.13	.17	.19	.07	.16	.19
Craftsmen, foremen, and kindred workers	.30	.42	.50	.16	.41	.54
Operatives and kindred workers	.69	1.05	1.23	.34	.76	.82
Private household workers	7.00	5.71	5.32	3.38	4.87	4.60
Service workers, except private household	1.92	2.27	2.32	.92	1.55	1.58
Farm laborers and foremen	2.44	2.14	2.55	4.49	2.61	2.47
Laborers, except farm and mine	2.44	2.92	2.96	.96	1.88	1.85

SOURCE: Computed from data from the 1940, 1950, and 1960 censuses of U.S. population.
[a] The "expected" proportion of Negroes in each occupational group is the proportion of Negroes in the total employed labor force.

creased only slightly, from .13 in 1940 to .17 in 1960. The ratio for professional and technical workers declined, from .33 in 1940 to .30 in 1960.

This decline is accounted for by a large decrease in Negro clergymen, from 17,102 in 1940 to 13,955 in 1960. The number of male clergymen per 10,000 population declined from 13.3 in 1940 to 7.4 in 1960 for Negroes but increased from 9.8 to 11.4 for whites. This decline in Negro clergymen reflects the passing from the scene of the older traditional minister, perhaps a declining interest in religion among Negro Americans, and increased opportunities for young

Negroes in more lucrative lines of work. Since most Negro clergymen in 1940 were poorly educated, poorly paid, and professional workers only in the extended sense, a decline in their numbers may be regarded as a gain for Negroes.

If clergymen are excluded from the professional and technical category, there was a slight increase in the ratio from .24 for 1940 to .27 for 1960. In contrast to males, the ratio for Negro females increased appreciably in each of the highest-level occupational categories, from .33 in 1940 to .55 in 1960 as professional and technical workers, and from .19 to .28 as managers, officials, and proprietors.

In spite of Negro gains in the 1940s and 1950s, both males and females in 1960 were far from proportionally represented in all of the white-collar occupational groups and as craftsmen and foremen. Furthermore, the recent rate of Negro increase in these occupations is not great enough to lead to occupational equality in the near future. For instance, assuming that the representation of Negro males as professional, technical, and kindred workers (excluding clergymen) were to continue to increase at the 1940–1960 rate, it would not be for *530 years* after 1960 (until the year 2490) that proportional representation would be attained. By the same calculations, proportional representation of Negro males would not be attained as managers, officials, and proprietors within 415 years and as sales workers not for 270 years. Since these projections extend several generations beyond the lifetime of Negroes now living, it is small wonder that Negroes imbued with the ideal of equality are less than satisfied with the recent pace of occupational gains. To be sure, neither Negroes nor whites are aware of the arithmetic of trends nor their harsh implications, but some Negroes may sense the rate of change. (The reader must be cautioned that these figures are projections, not predictions. Alterations in the rates of change probably will occur and we point to some of the conditions that may cause such changes. Nevertheless, the projections do dramatize the gap that remains.)

Small as the ratios were in the higher-level occupational

groups in 1960, they do not fully reveal the extent of inequality. Within each occupational group, Negroes were relatively concentrated in the lower-paying and lower-prestige occupations. For instance, the occupational group of professional, technical, and kindred workers includes such diverse occupations as physicians, engineers, school teachers, social workers, and medical and dental technicians. In 1960, only 11.4 percent of the employed Negro male professional, technical, and kindred workers were architects, dentists, engineers, lawyers, judges, physicians, and surgeons. In contrast, 31.4 percent of the employed white male professionals had these higher-paying occupations. In addition, the rate of increase of Negroes in the higher-level professional and technical occupations has generally been less (see Table 5). For instance, from 1940 to 1960 there was no increase in the representation of Negro males as physicians and surgeons or as college presidents, professors, and instructors, and the increase in Negro representation as dentists was very small. The big gains were in relatively low-paying semiprofessional occupations, such as welfare and recreation workers and medical and dental technicians.

TABLE 5. RATIO OF ACTUAL TO EXPECTED PROPORTION OF NEGRO MALES IN SELECTED OCCUPATIONS, UNITED STATES, 1940, 1950, AND 1960

	1940	1950	1960
Accountants and auditors	n.a.[a]	.04	.07
Architects	.05	.07	.10
Artists and art teachers	.08	.14	.20
Authors, editors, and reporters	.09	.09	.11
Bookkeepers	n.a.	.06	.12
Chemists	.06	.12	.24
Clergymen	1.48	1.31	.85
College presidents, professors, and instructors			
(not elsewhere classified)	.30	.30	.30
Dentists	.24	.24	.30
Designers and draftsmen	.01	.05	.13
Engineers			
—aeronautical	n.a.	.02	.07
—civil	.01	.05	.10
—electrical	.01	.03	.08

	1940	1950	1960
—mechanical	.01	.03	.05
Insurance agents and brokers	n.a.	.23	.18
Lawyers and judges	.07	.09	.12
Mail carriers	.54	.87	1.24
Medical and dental technicians	n.a.	.44	.95
Musicians and music teachers	.82	.86	.83
Natural scientists (not elsewhere classified)	n.a.	.16	.18
Pharmacists	.12	.16	.20
Physicians and surgeons	.25	.24	.24
Real estate agents and brokers	.13	.20	.20
Salaried managers, officials, and proprietors (not elsewhere classified)			
—in manufacturing	n.a.	.03	.05
—in retail and wholesale trade	n.a.	.13	.11
—in finance, insurance, and real estate	n.a.	.10	.12
Salesmen and sales clerks			
—in manufacturing	n.a.	.05	.06
—in wholesale trade	n.a.	.05	.06
—in retail trade	n.a.	.20	.25
Self-employed managers, officials, and proprietors (not elsewhere classified)			
—in construction	n.a.	.20	.21
—in manufacturing	n.a.	.06	.10
—in wholesale trade	n.a.	.17	.24
—in eating and drinking places	n.a.	.46	.45
—in other retail trade	n.a.	.19	.18
Social scientists	n.a.	.15	.19
Social, welfare, and recreation workers	n.a.	.73	1.17
Teachers (not elsewhere classified)	.63	.76	.77

SOURCE: Computed from data from the 1940, 1950, and 1960 censuses of U.S. population.

[a] Not available.

Not only are Negroes concentrated in the lower-paying occupations; they generally earn less than whites in the same occupations. The 1959 median earnings of white and non-white males in selected occupations are shown in Table 6. The gap between whites and nonwhites was generally less in governmental occupations such as postal workers, firemen, and policemen. For the seven occupations of this type in the table, the average ratio of nonwhite to white median earnings was .92, whereas for the other occupations the average was

TABLE 6. RATIO OF NONWHITE TO WHITE MEDIAN EARNINGS OF MALES
IN SELECTED OCCUPATIONS, UNITED STATES, 1959

Occupation	Ratio of nonwhite to white	Occupation	Ratio of nonwhite to white
Electrical and electronics technicians	.98	Secondary school teachers	.76
Firemen, fire protection	.96	Foremen (not elsewhere classified)	.74
Mail carriers	.96	Compositors and type-setters	.73
Postal clerks	.95	Automobile mechanics and repairmen	.71
Policemen and detectives	.95	Dentists	.70
Aeronautical engineers	.94	Linemen and servicemen, telegraph, telephone, and power	.69
Electrical engineers	.91		
Inspectors, public administration	.90	Laborers, except farm and mine	.69
Bookkeepers	.90	Musicians and music teachers	.67
Designers and draftsmen	.88	Painters, construction and maintenance	.64
Airplane mechanics and repairmen	.88	Clergymen	.64
Mechanical engineers	.88	Barbers	.64
Bus drivers	.87	Insurance agents, brokers, and underwriters	.63
Electricians	.86	Salesmen and sales clerks (not elsewhere classified)	.63
Civil engineers	.86		
Accountants and auditors	.84	Brickmasons, stonemasons, and tile setters	.61
Officials and administrators, public administration	.83	Truck and tractor drivers	.59
Office machine operators	.83	Cement and concrete finishers	.59
Elementary school teachers	.82	Plumbers and pipe fitters	.58
Medical and dental technicians	.80	Plasterers	.56
Radio and television mechanics and repairmen	.79	Carpenters	.55
Chemists	.78	Farm laborers, wage workers	.52
College professors and instructors	.77	Physicians and surgeons	.39
Mine operatives and laborers (not elsewhere classified)	.77	Farmers and farm managers	.33
Shipping and receiving clerks	.77		

SOURCE: Computed from data from *U.S. Census of Population: 1960,* Final
Report PC(2)-7B, Table 1 (U.S. Bureau of the Census, Washington, D.C.).

only .72. Present-day discrimination in government employment, where it exists, more often takes the form of exclusion
than of lower pay. Even at the state and local levels, wages
and salaries are fairly well standardized, and Negroes and
whites with similar jobs and similar seniority are usually paid
about the same. Highly trained Negro workers, such as engineers and electronics technicians, who are employed mainly
by private industry also are paid almost as much as their
white counterparts. In contrast, an appreciable earnings gap
existed in 1959 between Negroes and whites in most manual
occupations and in those occupations in which Negroes serve
other Negroes as entrepreneurs or as employees of Negro
institutions. Some, but not all, of the Negro-white disparity
in earnings within occupations is due to greater unemployment of Negroes in most occupations.

The Negro-white occupational gap obviously is still very
wide, and it is closing so slowly that it will not disappear
within the next century unless the rate of Negro gains
sharply accelerates. Some acceleration, especially at the highest levels, is likely and may already have occurred since 1960.
The increased race consciousness of Negroes is making the
opening of higher-level government jobs to Negroes a political necessity and is making the hiring of Negroes by private
firms requisite to the attraction and holding of a large Negro
clientele. There will be some discrimination in favor of Negroes, but unless it becomes more widespread than seems
probable, near equality in occupational status must await
near equality in occupational qualifications. As we point out
above, near equality in qualifications is at least several decades away.

The Income Gap

Until recently, the moderate closing of the occupational
gap between employed Negroes and whites was accompanied
by a similar narrowing of the income gap. The income gap
closed appreciably during World War II but very slowly and

erratically during the postwar period. White and nonwhite median family incomes in constant (1965) dollars are shown for each year from 1947 to 1965 in Figure 2. Incomes for both races went up steeply during the period, but the ratio of the nonwhite to the white median hardly changed; it was exactly the same in 1965 as it was in 1955. The absolute gap between the white and nonwhite medians increased. The data in Table 7 on the median income of individuals show greater improvement in the relative standing of nonwhites. However, these data are only for persons *with* income, and since a greater percentage of Negro than of white adult males had no income, the comparison of family incomes is more meaningful. Nevertheless, it is important that the ratio of Negro to white median income of males with income did not increase from 1949 to 1959.

TABLE 7. MEDIAN INCOME OF PERSONS WITH INCOME, BY RACE AND SEX, UNITED STATES, 1949 AND 1959

	Negro	White	Ratio of Negro to white
Both sexes			
1949	961	2,058	.47
1959	1,519	3,026	.50
Male			
1949	1,356	2,582	.53
1959	2,254	4,338	.52
Female			
1949	703	1,139	.62
1959	905	1,509	.60

SOURCE: *U.S. Census of Population: 1960,* Final Report PC(1)-1D, p. 578 (U.S. Bureau of the Census, Washington, D.C.).

The slower rate of income gains as compared to occupational gains of Negroes is largely accounted for by (1) an increase in the difference between white and nonwhite unemployment rates and (2) an increase in the income gap between lower-level and other occupations. The ratio of non-

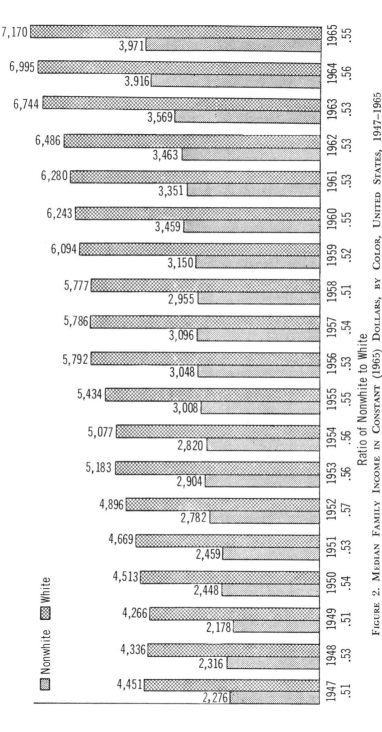

Ratio of Nonwhite to White

FIGURE 2. MEDIAN FAMILY INCOME IN CONSTANT (1965) DOLLARS, BY COLOR, UNITED STATES, 1947–1965. SOURCE: Computed from data reported annually by the U.S. Bureau of the Census in *Current Population Reports*, Series P-60.

white to white percentage of workers unemployed increased from 1.18 in 1940, to 1.73 in 1950, to 1.85 in 1960. The absolute differences between the percentages for the same three years were 2.6, 3.3, and 4.0. Mechanization of industrial processes that eliminated many jobs in occupations in which Negroes are concentrated largely accounts for this widening of the unemployment gap.

Demand for unskilled and semiskilled labor has declined more rapidly than Negroes have acquired the education and training requisite to upgrading into expanding lines of work, and unless Negro education and skills improve more rapidly than is likely, the difference between Negro and white unemployment rates is likely to grow with further mechanization and automation. If so, the effects may offset many past as well as future occupational gains. The occupational advances of Negro workers after 1940 were largely into intermediate-level jobs that are subject to elimination by automation. The largest movement of Negro workers was into the occupational group of operatives and kindred workers, a category which is already hard hit by technological unemployment. In 1960, 6.4 percent of the males and 9.9 percent of the females in this occupational group were unemployed—higher unemployment than among any other class of workers except laborers. (Only part, however, was technological unemployment; much of it was caused by reduced production in some industries.) Many kinds of skilled workers also are being displaced by mechanization, although Negro craftsmen generally are more secure than Negro operatives. Unemployment in 1960 was relatively low among clerical and kindred workers, the other occupational group into which Negroes moved in large numbers. However, clerical jobs appear to be next in line to feel the impact of automation. Most of the occupational gains of Negroes during the past quarter of a century, in fact, are vulnerable to automation and other technological changes.

The reduced demand for unskilled labor has prevented incomes of unskilled workers from rising as fast as incomes of other workers. Wage and salary income of unskilled workers was little higher in 1959 than in 1949. Wages and salaries in general rose steeply during the decade, so the gap between unskilled and other workers widened. Since Negroes are overrepresented in unskilled work, this change tended to widen the income gap between Negroes and whites even though Negro representation increased at the higher occupational levels during the same period.

For similar reasons, the closing of the educational gap during the 1950s was not accompanied by a corresponding closing of the economic gap. The ratio of nonwhite to white median years of school completed by persons 25 years old and older increased from .71 in 1950 to .75 in 1960. Because the income gap is to a large extent a reflection of the educational gap, one might have expected similar marked improvement in the relative economic status of Negroes during the 1950s. Yet such improvement did not occur, because the economic gap between all poorly educated workers and others widened and Negroes remained highly represented among the poorly educated. In 1949, the median income of males who had completed one to four years of elementary school was 43 percent of the median income of those who had completed high school and was 31 percent of the median income of those who had completed four or more years of college. By 1959, these percentages had declined to 34 and 24.

Negro Americans are on a treadmill. They must keep gaining on whites in education and occupation simply to stay the same distance behind in income. Undoubtedly, this condition adversely affects Negro morale. Many Negroes find it increasingly difficult to get and keep jobs, and many who manage to remain employed most of the time do not share in the general increase in real income in the United States. While their own economic condition becomes worse or improves only slowly, their appetite for a more affluent style of life is whetted by direct observation of increased consumption by other Americans (both whites and the growing number of middle-class Negroes) and by increased exposure to the mass media of communication. Their feelings of deprivation increase even if their absolute economic condition improves.

The increased sense of deprivation of poorly educated Negroes is not unique but is shared by many poorly educated and unskilled whites. However, the consequences of Negro discontent are different. Negroes tend to define their troubles in racial terms, especially since the recent increased publicity given to the struggle for equal rights. The plight of the large percentage of Negroes who are poorly educated and unskilled has appreciable effects upon other Negroes. Self-employed Negro businessmen and professionals are dependent upon other Negroes and can hope to improve their economic condition only as the economic condition of the entire Negro population improves. Middle-class Negroes employed in the integrated economy have less reason to be concerned about the plight of poor Negroes, but whether they care or not, their fates are linked in important ways. Middle-class Negroes often must live in neighborhoods with lower-class Negroes, send their children to schools in which most of the pupils come from lower-class families, and in general have more frequent and closer contacts with lower-class people than do middle-class whites. An increasing number of middle-class Negroes owe their jobs to the political influence and buying power either of the entire Negro population or of the local Negro community. In addition, these people know that whites are likely to judge them on the basis of stereotypes that reflect the characteristics of the lower class. Therefore, a condition that adversely affects any segment of the Negro population has some adverse effects on all. Negroes are apparently becoming more sensitive to this fact, and the plight of unskilled workers causes some unrest among all classes.

As we suggest above, improvement in the relative occupational status of Negro Americans since the beginning of World War II seems, to a large extent, to be an outgrowth of a high level of nationwide prosperity, a high rate of economic growth, and changes in the occupation structure generating many upper- and intermediate-level jobs. The evidence for this reasoning is convincing if not conclusive. For example, Negroes generally made their greatest occupational gains in lines of work in which the number of jobs increased most rapidly (Glenn *d*, p. 112). Their relative economic status improved during years of rapid economic growth and generally declined or was static during years of little or no economic growth. These facts might lead one to conclude that future Negro gains are largely contingent upon continued economic growth and changes in the economic structure. Such changes probably are necessary for Negro gains, but they are hardly sufficient, and there is reason to believe that they will be less beneficial to Negroes than they have been. Rapid economic growth in the past has helped Negroes mainly by reducing unemployment. The economic status of Negroes has generally risen during years of full employment in the total labor force and fallen during years of high unemployment. Now, however, a rapid rate of economic growth does not reduce unemployment as much as it once did; high rates of economic growth and high rates of unemployment recently have occurred together. For instance, the rate of economic growth in the United States from 1958 to 1959 was about 8.5 percent, well above the average for the previous decade, but unemployment in 1959 was 5.5 percent, also well above the average for the previous decade. (The rate of economic growth is defined roughly as the annual percentage increase in the value, in constant dollars, of all goods and services purchased for final use.)

In the future, unemployment may actually increase during years of rapid economic growth, and if so, rapid expansion of the economy may no longer tend to improve the relative status of Negroes. Furthermore, the opening of new jobs at the higher and intermediate occupational levels may no longer be greatly beneficial to the Negro population as a whole if there is an accompanying large decrease in jobs at the lower levels. The number of Negroes displaced from lower-level jobs may be larger than the number who are qualified to take advantage of openings at intermediate and higher levels. In short, economic and occupational trends of the future may benefit Negroes appreciably only if their occupational qualifications improve very rapidly. And the improvement of Negro occupational qualifications depends largely, although not completely, upon improvement in the quantity and quality of Negro education. The obstacles to rapid improvement in Negro education are formidable; and perhaps the obstacles to rapid improvement of the occupational qualifications of adult Negroes who have completed their formal education are even greater. Therefore, the relative economic status of Negroes may drop below its present level within the next few years. Only unforeseen developments could bring about a rapid increase in the near future.

Interrelations among Education, Occupation, and Income

The gap between Negroes and whites in the amount of formal education accounts for much, but not all, of the occupation and income gaps. Negroes and whites with the same amount of schooling differ greatly in their incomes and occupations (see Tables 8 and 9). The differences are due in part to persisting discrimination and to the handicaps under which self-employed Negroes work. But, as noted in Chapter

TABLE 8. RATIO OF NONWHITE TO WHITE MEDIAN INCOME OF MALES 25
YEARS OLD AND OLDER, BY EDUCATIONAL LEVEL, UNITED STATES,
1949 AND 1959

School years completed	1949	1959
none	.68	.66
1–4	.54	.80
5–7	.70	.73
8	.72	.73
1–3 high school	.67	.65
4 high school	.68	.68
1–3 college	.64	.66
4 or more college	.59	.62

SOURCES: Computed from data from U.S. Census of Population: 1950, Special Report PE No. 5B, Table 12, and U.S. Census of Population: 1960, Final Report, PC(1)-1D, p. 590 (Washington, D.C., U.S. Bureau of the Census).

TABLE 9. INDEX OF OCCUPATIONAL DISSIMILARITY[a] BETWEEN NONWHITE
AND WHITE MALES 25–44 YEARS OLD, BY EDUCATIONAL LEVEL,
UNITED STATES, 1950 AND 1960

Years of school completed	25–34 years old, 1950	35–44 years old, 1960	25–34 years old, 1960
Less than 5	22	19	18
5–7	26	27	26
8	29	27	27
1–3 high school	29	31	28
4 high school	32	31	31
1–3 college	30	30	26
4 or more college	11	9	6

SOURCE: Computed from data from the 1950 and 1960 censuses of U.S. population.

[a] The index of occupational dissimilarity is the percentage of nonwhite workers who would have to move from one occupational category to another in order for the nonwhite and white occupational distributions to be equal. Nine broad occupational categories were used to compute the index values shown here.

5, Negroes and whites with the same number of years of school are frequently not equally qualified. All these factors combine to create a particularly stubborn obstacle to Negro achievement and a heavy burden to Negro morale. The inequality between Negroes and whites with the same amount of formal education is perhaps even more burdensome to morale than the economic inequality that can be attributed to differences in the amount of schooling.

The gaps in both occupation and income are generally greater at upper educational levels. For instance, in 1949 and in 1959, nonwhite males with from five to eight years of school fared better relative to their white counterparts than did nonwhite males at any higher educational level. In 1959, the biggest gap between nonwhite and white incomes was at the highest educational level. This difference perhaps in part reflects a greater difference in average qualifications at higher levels. The relatively small gap at the *lower* levels reflects the fact that the quality of formal education has little relevance to qualifications for many of unskilled and semiskilled jobs.

The greater income and occupational disparity at the

higher educational levels is an additional reason why the increased average educational status of Negroes probably has led to increased discontent and feelings of deprivation. Not only is the well-educated Negro better able to perceive the status gap between himself and his white educational counterpart—he also perceives a wider gap. And the wider gap probably contributes to the restiveness and urge to protest that seem to be engendered by increased education.

If the status differences between Negroes and whites with the same amount of education were diminishing rapidly, Negro discontent might be less. However, changes from 1950 to 1960 were small. Ratios of nonwhite to white median income of males in 1949 and in 1959 are shown for each of eight educational levels in Table 8. The ratio increased from 1949 to 1959 at five levels, decreased at two levels, and stayed the same at one. However, only one change—the increase in the relative status of nonwhites with one to four years of school—was large enough to be important, and this increase came about not because the median income of nonwhites increased steeply but because the median income of white males at this educational level *declined* in constant dollars during the decade. Nonwhite income at the one-through-four-year educational level was very low in 1949, and it probably was kept from dropping by relief payments and the extension of minimum-wage legislation.

There was little change during the 1950s in the relative economic standing of nonwhite males with high school education, and the increase was small among the college educated. However, the incomes of well-educated nonwhites did rise in relation to the incomes of whites with less education— one aspect of the general widening of the economic gap between the well educated and the poorly educated. For instance, in 1949 the median nonwhite male with four or more years of college had an income only 3 percent higher than the income of the median white male with an eighth-grade education. By 1959 this difference had risen to 20 percent. Even so, in 1959 the median income of nonwhite males with four or more years of college did not yet equal the median income of white males with one to three years of high school.

The data in Table 9 give a rough indication of the occupational status of nonwhite males compared to white males in 1950 and 1960. The index of dissimilarity reported is simply the percentage of nonwhites who would have to move from one occupational category to another in order for the distribution of nonwhites and whites among nine broad occupational categories to be the same. Therefore, the higher the index, the wider is the occupational gap. The occupational categories from which the data have been computed are the same as those used in the U.S. census, except that clerical and sales workers are combined into a single category and professional and technical workers are combined with managers, officials, and proprietors. The combination of groups similar in prestige and incomes results in nine categories that form a hierarchy, in prestige and desirability, of the occupations they include. Crude though it is, the index of occupational dissimilarity correlates highly with more complex and refined indexes of occupational differences. Its major weakness is that it does not reflect the considerable vertical differences between nonwhites and whites *within* the occupational groups. This weakness could not easily be overcome because the Bureau of the Census did not tabulate complete data on detailed occupations by educational level. Consequently, the index understates the extent of nonwhite disadvantage, but it is still a convenient way of summarizing such statistics.

The occupational difference between nonwhite and white males who were 25 through 34 years old in 1950 (a category that included approximately the same people who were 35 through 44 years old in 1960) changed very little during the decade. The biggest decline in the index was among those with four years or more of college, and the decline is not clear-cut evidence of an increase in opportunity for Negroes. The change could stem from differences in the career patterns of nonwhites and whites with a college education. Since more whites began their careers in the top category, white upward movement was more often within the category and did not affect the distribution of white workers among the nine categories.

The difference between the index values for workers who were 25 through 34 years old in 1950 and those of the same age in 1960 is greater. The index declined some at each level of schooling except the five-to-seven-year level, and it declined appreciably at the college levels. A much larger percentage of college-educated young nonwhite males was in professional and technical occupations in 1960, and the non-white increase was greater than the white increase. Again, however, there is no clear-cut evidence of increased opportunity. The higher relative status of the younger nonwhites could be the consequence of improvement in their qualifications and in the quality of Negro education.

Much of the discrimination-caused difference in status between whites and nonwhites with the same amount of education is likely to disappear within a decade or two. This trend is especially evident at the higher educational levels. Many corporations are recruiting Negroes for fairly high positions because it has become good public relations policy to do so. Likewise, many colleges and universities are adding Negro faculty and staff members either because of the shortage of qualified white personnel or to show a lack of discrimination. Appointment of Negroes to high posts in the federal government and to many state agencies in the North and West has become good politics. Such lowering of the color bar is as yet hardly more than "tokenism" and will not in itself go far toward solving the economic problems of Negroes. However, conspicuous employment of Negroes has become prevalent enough within the past two or three years so that the demand for competent and personable Negro college graduates probably exceeds the supply. The appearance of well-qualified Negroes in conspicuous positions of responsibility has diverse effects. White co-workers who never before associated with Negroes in an egalitarian setting—perhaps who never before associated with Negroes—have an opportunity to observe the

Negro as a man and react to him as a person. Whites whose image of the Negro is bound by stereotypes find that the stereotypes do not stand up under daily observations in the work setting. Negroes whose lives were lived out in a world of Negroes find broader horizons and gain greater familiarity with middle-class white standards and styles.

At the lower educational levels, the extension and more stringent enforcement of antidiscrimination legislation may lessen discrimination, and the widespread use of boycotts and demonstrations may be even more effective in bringing down the color bar. However, lessened job discrimination depends upon continued favorable economic conditions whereby interests of large segments of the white population will not be threatened by Negro gains. If upper- and intermediate-level jobs do not increase fast enough to provide job opportunities for almost all qualified workers of both races, white resistance to Negro advancement probably will stiffen and discrimination may increase. The sober fact is that, in spite of recent gains in Negro power, any large segment of the white population still has an advantage over Negroes. White customers, with their greater buying power, could, if they wished, influence the employment practices of business firms more than Negroes. Any sizable number of white voters, properly distributed, could offset the political influence of Negroes. In short, any large segment of the white population that so desired could use the same means to increase discrimination that Negroes are now using to lessen it.

Nevertheless, it seems unlikely that white resistance will now reverse the trend away from discrimination. Only a business depression or other major disruption of the economy could make Negro advancement a serious threat to a large number of white workers, except perhaps in a few localities in which the Negro population is relatively large. Furthermore, social and cultural change, once under way, gathers momentum that enables it to continue in the face of increased opposing influences. For instance, the more widespread acceptance of egalitarian values during recent years would make it hard to justify increased discrimination. Whites who would gain from greater discrimination no doubt could justify it to themselves, but egalitarian values would deter many other whites from supporting it. Even if there is no real threat, some white workers may *feel* threatened and oppose the trend toward equal opportunity, but their resistance is not likely to halt the trend.

It might be possible to eliminate the more important kinds of discrimination within the next few years, but the quality of Negro education cannot be improved so rapidly, and Negro-white status differences will persist for a long time. A shortage of skills and educational qualifications may soon become a much greater obstacle to Negro advancement than a dearth of available jobs. Indeed, such may already be the case.

The Role of Organized Labor

Organized labor has played both beneficial and detrimental roles in Negro economic and occupational status. During the past few decades the detrimental effects have decreased and the beneficial ones have increased, but union discrimination remains a major obstacle to Negro advancement.

Countervailing influences have blunted and diverted the ability of organized labor either to hinder or to help. On the negative side, many white union members are recruited from some of the more prejudiced parts of the white population. Although the evidence is not clear-cut and consistent, it seems that manual workers are somewhat more anti-Negro on the average than white-collar workers.* Members of ethnic minorities and migrants from the rural South, numerous among union members, are also prone to strong anti-Negro

---

* But the presumed greater prejudice of "working-class" people may be more apparent than real. Manual workers express prejudice less subtly and their rationalizations are less sophisticated. They do not so clearly understand the purpose of paper-and-pencil tests and interviewers' questions that are designed to measure prejudice and are more likely to make "prejudiced" responses than are white-collar workers with basically similar attitudes.

sentiments. In general, manual workers are more directly in competition with large numbers of Negroes and may feel threatened by Negro advancement. These union members, motivated by their own perceived interests, tend to exclude Negroes from unions or to discriminate against them if they are admitted. Since craft unions are more fraternal than industrial unions, membership in them more clearly implies social equality; the incentive of prejudiced members to exclude Negroes has therefore been especially strong.

On the positive side, intellectuals in the labor movement have espoused the ideal of racial equality, but their liberalism affects the formal policies of international unions more than the practices of locals. No doubt the international policy has been filtering down to the local level, although the extent of such influence is not fully documented. Egalitarian values are more apparent in industrial than craft unions, but decreased discrimination in them may be motivated by self-interest and necessity as well as ethical conviction. The egalitarian ideology may be as much a reflection of practice as a molder of it. Industrial unions, whose members are largely semiskilled and unskilled, often organized industries in which a large number of Negroes were already employed, and in order to attain their objectives, they had to be inclusive in their membership. Before Negroes were admitted to many unions, management used Negroes as strikebreakers, and it was in the interest of some industrial unions to lower racial bars. Craft unions, in contrast, organized workers by specific occupations rather than by industry, and few Negroes were employed in the typical craft occupations. Since craft-union membership was skilled, unskilled Negroes could not be used as strikebreakers against them; craft unions thus had no self-interest in lowering racial bars. It is not surprising, therefore, that the Congress of Industrial Organizations (CIO) espoused a policy of nondiscrimination when it was formed in 1935, whereas most craft unions in the American Federation of Labor (AFL) continued to discriminate.

Although Negro and white manual workers compete for

jobs, they have many interests in common, and their cooperation in the labor movement can be mutually advantageous.
Both benefit from industrial expansion that creates more jobs
and from improvements in wages, fringe benefits, and working conditions. Both are threatened by automation, retarded
economic growth, and antilabor legislation. While these
common interests and concerns have not led to a high degree
of solidarity between Negro and white workers, organized
labor and Negroes have occasionally formed effective political coalitions. A few such liberal alliances have been formed
in parts of the South; prospects of further ones are provoking
segregationists, especially the White Citizens Councils, to
expend considerable effort to foster anti-Negro feelings
among union members in order to prevent such alliances
(Marshall, pp. 384–385). Since most Southern workers probably have stronger race consciousness than class consciousness, a general Southern coalition of Negroes and unions is
unlikely in the near future.

Government action against discrimination has tended to
make organized labor deal more favorably with Negroes.
About half of the states have legislation specifically prohibiting discrimination in unions, even though effective enforcement is rare. Some federal labor legislation also prohibits
discrimination, but some does not. For instance, the Railway
Labor Act and the Wagner-Connery Act require unions that
are granted exclusive bargaining rights to represent all workers fairly but do not require them to admit Negroes to
membership; their effects upon discriminatory union practices have thus been small (Marshall, p. 385). The National
Labor Relations Board has used its regulatory powers only to
a limited extent to prevent discrimination. It has threatened
to revoke the certification of discriminating unions, but it has
not done so (Marshall, p. 386).

The most effective governmental action against union
discrimination has been taken by Presidential committees set
up to police employment practices of firms with government
contracts. These include President Roosevelt's wartime Fair

Employment Practices Committee, President Eisenhower's Committee on Government Contracts, and President Kennedy's Committee on Equal Employment Opportunity (CEEO). The first two of these, which applied their sanctions to employers only, had only an indirect effect upon union practices. The CEEO, however, was directed to "cause any labor union . . . [which] is or may be engaged in work under government contracts to cooperate with and to comply in the implementation of the purposes of the order [which forbade discrimination in work done under government contracts]." As a result of the committee's activity, a few unions have integrated their locals in the South and a few additional jobs have opened to Negroes. The personal efforts of Presidents Kennedy and Johnson have been at least as effective as the activities of the committee. President Kennedy persuaded unions that include 90 percent of the AFL-CIO's membership to sign pledges to comply with his executive order prohibiting discrimination in work done under government contracts. The short-run effect of these pledges upon practice is not clear, but the long-run consequences may be important.

Government pressure, unfavorable publicity, and other influences have fostered considerable change in union racial policies, if not in practices. In 1930, at least twenty-two unions officially barred Negroes from membership, but the number fell to thirteen in 1943, to nine in 1949, and to two in 1963. Discrimination on the unofficial level did not decline correspondingly, however, and continues in numerous unions—for example, by refusal to admit Negroes to apprenticeship programs, by agreements not to sponsor Negroes for membership, and by rigging examinations to refuse Negroes journeymen status. Auxiliary Negro locals, controlled by white locals, were once numerous, but most were integrated with white locals or given "separate but equal" status before the Landrum-Griffin Act of 1959 made it possible for Negro employees to bring legal action to abolish auxiliary locals. However, "separate but equal" Negro locals are still common in the South. In some trades, the existence of separate locals denies Negroes equal job opportunities, but in others Negroes have protected territories and therefore have little to gain from integration. Some Negroes feel they have greater freedom of action, especially in pursuing nonunion interests, by having their own locals (Marshall, pp. 379–380). However, younger Negroes tend to oppose segregation on principle, and greater agitation for integration of locals is to be expected.

Most remaining discrimination is in craft unions, where it is probably rooted primarily in the desire of present members to reduce competition by keeping membership low. In this situation, race prejudice as such is not a basic motivation for action, but it is manipulated to achieve economic objectives. Many craft unions limit membership and the number of persons in their apprenticeship programs to create a shortage of qualified workers and thus maintain high wages and job security. Consequently, it has been difficult for many whites as well as for Negroes to enter certain trades. Some craft unions allegedly practice nepotism; one must have close ties to a union member to become a member or an apprentice. In those crafts, Negroes may be discriminated against not because of race but because they have no relatives or close friends in the union.

Whatever the basis, the exclusion of Negroes from craft unions and segregation into separate locals with limited access to jobs are major obstacles to Negro advancement. Most Negro Americans are now denied entry into business, professional, technical, and many clerical and sales jobs because they are poorly educated. The only well-paying and rapidly expanding lines of work that do not require a high level of formal education are the skilled trades, and Negro entry into these occupations is impeded by union policy, tradition, and the present makeup of membership.

Negroes are now well represented in semiskilled work and in the industrial unions, but the importance of this kind of work is declining. Mechanization has eliminated some semiskilled jobs of many types and will soon eliminate others, thus undermining the influence of unions that organize semi-skilled workers. The total experienced civilian labor force increased by 15 percent from 1950 to 1960, but semiskilled workers increased by only about 9 percent. Some types of skilled workers were also hard hit by mechanization, but skilled workers as a whole increased almost as much as the total labor force—by about 13 percent. Technological changes have increased the demand for such skilled workers as electricians, aircraft mechanics, television repairmen, and the like. In fact, there is an acute shortage of workers in some skills. Median earnings of skilled workers in 1959 were well above the median for the entire labor force and well above the medians for clerical and sales workers. In short, skilled work is almost the only kind of work for which a college education is not required that has a relatively bright future. To an increasing extent, the skilled trades offer the greatest hope for above-average income and style of life to the man with no college training.

Breaching the barrier to the skilled trades is the one possible major breakthrough in Negro occupations that is not dependent on drastically improved quantity and quality of education. Of course, some formal education is required for skilled work, but thousands of Negro youths have the basic education and aptitudes for successful apprenticeship. Many have acquired marketable skills through vocational training in high school, although too often such training is in obsolescent lines of work. Therefore, Negroes are in a position to make appreciable gains whenever restrictive union practices are discontinued. But past experience suggests that union discrimination will be discontinued only under strong government pressures. More legislation and executive orders that prohibit discrimination by unions are probably forthcoming, but their effective enforcement will be difficult and may be politically inexpedient. White craftsmen outnumber all Negro workers and, like Negroes, are highly concentrated in populous states with many electoral votes. These whites can be expected to use political influence to oppose government removal of racial barriers in unions, to protect themselves from competition from Negroes. Or, they may meet the Negro "threat" through tokenism, that is, by admitting enough Negroes to lessen charges of discrimination but not enough to reduce appreciably the jobs available to whites. Therefore, the immediate prospects for large Negro gains in skilled work do not seem bright.

7

Business and the Professions

Business

Many "solutions" have been offered for improving the status of Negroes, and separatism is a recurrent theme. It is argued that efforts to incorporate Negroes fully into the economy are doomed to failure, that at best they result in maintaining a system of categorical inferiority and economic vulnerability. The development of an independent economy has been proposed as an alternative. In such an economy, Negro enterprises would manufacture, distribute, wholesale, and retail the goods consumed by Negroes, and Negro establishments would provide needed services. Negro workers would then find jobs at all levels in segregated businesses. As a result, the Negro occupational structure would be separate from but parallel to the white occupational structure and would come to resemble it. There would be roughly the same proportion of professionals and big and small businesses in the two interlocked economies. Negroes would attain economic independence, since few would be dependent upon whites for employment. The days of subservience to white employers would be over.

The belief in a completely separate economy is illusory, although even today it has some proponents, including the Black Muslims. However, many Negro businessmen who realize that a completely separate economy is not feasible believe that development of Negro business is a way to achieve economic progress. During the 1930s and 1940s, they advocated the "double-duty dollar": the dollar spent at a Negro-owned store or service establishment that yields the extra benefits of jobs for Negroes and race advancement. Although the doctrine has its attractions for a striving people seeking ways of expressing solidarity, not much has been achieved; a very small percentage of Negro workers are employed by Negro enterprises. Negro business in the United States has had a dismal history, and it may have an even more dismal future. It may be the weakest sector of a thriving economy.

In 1950, there were about 42,500 self-employed male Negro businessmen in the United States. In 1960, there were only about 32,400—a decrease of 24 percent. The number declined in all regions, including the West where the Negro population nearly doubled during the decade, and the number of self-employed Negro businessmen for each 10,000 Negro population fell sharply in each region (see Table 10). The decrease may have been due chiefly to the elimination of weaker and smaller establishments, so that the total volume of Negro business probably did not decline proportionally.

TABLE 10. NUMBER OF SELF-EMPLOYED MALE BUSINESSMEN PER 10,000 POPULATION, BY RACE AND REGION, UNITED STATES, 1950 AND 1960

	Negro		White	
	1950	*1960*	*1950*	*1960*
United States	28	18	158	102
Northeast	38	18	174	95
North Central	37	18	143	91
South	23	16	149	118
West	47	24	177	114

SOURCE: Computed from data from the 1950 and 1960 censuses of U.S. population.

However, most surviving Negro businesses in 1960 were small operations.

To draw upon Census data for business earnings, we must use information on nonwhites rather than specifically on Negroes. According to the Census, less than a third of male nonwhite self-employed businessmen in 1959 earned $5,000 or more; about 8 percent earned $10,000 or more. But almost a third of all nonwhite businessmen were not Negroes, and these other nonwhites probably account for a disproportionately large part of high earnings. Thirty percent of nonwhite independent businessmen earned less than $2,000 in 1959, and no doubt a larger percentage of Negroes fell in this lowest category. In contrast, only 12 percent of white independent businessmen earned less than $2,000. About 25 percent of white independent businessmen earned $10,000 or more, compared with the 8 percent indicated for nonwhites.

The trends that reduced the number of independent Negro businessmen during the 1950s also brought about an almost proportionate decrease (23 percent) in independent white businessmen. Table 10 shows that the number of self-employed businessmen per 10,000 population dropped in all regions among whites as well as among Negroes. Furthermore, the percentage increase in income was apparently no greater for white businessmen than for Negroes. It seems that Negroes fared about as well in competition with small white businesses in 1960 as in 1950. But small business in general is losing ground against large corporate enterprise. The independent retailer is being displaced by the chain store, the discount house, and the large department store. The fundamental handicaps of Negro businessmen are those that hamper all small businessmen, and the Negro entrepreneur is characteristically a small entrepreneur.

In addition, however, the Negro businessman has several unique disadvantages. Whereas white owners of stores and of many service establishments cater to all races, Negro businessmen, with few exceptions, can hope to attract only a Negro clientele. The potential clientele of the Negro businessman is relatively small and relatively poor. For instance, in a city where Negroes make up a fifth of the population, they may have little more than a tenth of the total buying power. The white merchant has a better chance to benefit from economies of scale. His larger and more affluent clientele generates a larger volume of sales; he can operate on a smaller profit margin and can thus undersell the small merchant. The larger enterprise can stock a wider variety of goods and can afford to extend credit more liberally and, because it has better investigative facilities, with less risk. Therefore, the white merchant attracts Negro customers, who, like other buyers, usually shop where they get the most for their money, where they find the widest selection of goods and services, or where they can get credit.

Most businesses in Negro neighborhoods are convenience goods stores and service establishments. The grocery and drug stores sell frequently purchased and relatively inexpensive goods, and their accessible locations make up for high prices and a limited variety of merchandise. The service establishments provide facilities that white establishments are unwilling to offer. Restaurants, taverns, barber shops, beauty parlors, cleaning establishments, movie theaters, and funeral parlors are numerous. The last are perhaps the most prosperous of small Negro businesses. Since most white-owned funeral parlors do not compete for Negro funerals, which they fear would diminish their white patronage, Negro establishments have a virtual monopoly on Negro burials.

Except for such service establishments as funeral parlors and beauty shops, many businesses in Negro neighborhoods are owned by whites. For instance, in the early 1940s more than half of the businesses in Negro neighborhoods in Chicago were owned by whites, and these establishments received more than 90 percent of all money spent by Negroes in these areas (Drake and Cayton, p. 438). The failure of Negro business to compete with white-owned businesses in areas such as Harlem and the Chicago Black Belt, where the volume of sales is large, suggests that Negro businesses are handicapped by factors other than their relatively small and poor clientele. There are at least three reasons for this condition, and as we have so often observed, each factor feeds on itself and reinforces the others. First, because of their high failure rate, Negro businessmen are considered poor credit risks and have difficulty getting capital for expansion. In turn, their inability to expand keeps them small and ineffective competitors and makes them more likely to fail. When they do fail, their failure becomes a reason for loans to be denied to other Negro businesses. Second, white real estate owners generally choose to rent business buildings to whites, so Negroes rarely are able to find preferred locations. Finally, because of the insignificant size of Negro business in the past, and because until recently almost no Negroes held managerial positions in white-owned businesses, Negroes lack a business tradition and have less business experience and knowledge than whites.

Negroes have been even less successful in wholesaling, manufacturing, and finance than in retailing and service. Most of the few successful Negro manufacturing firms make cosmetics, caskets, or embalming supplies for the Negro market. Negroes got an early start in the Negro cosmetic industry and still manufacture a sizable proportion of preparations to straighten hair and lighten complexion. (The first successful hair-straightener was invented by a Negro woman.) The monopoly of Negro burials and a preference of many undertakers to purchase supplies from other Negroes contributed to the success of a few manufacturers of caskets and embalming supplies. A small Negro-owned record company in Chicago is a rare example of a manufacturing firm whose products are consumed by whites and compete in the open market.

Negroes have achieved their most substantial business success in insurance, in part because of past discriminatory actions by white companies that refused to insure Negroes on prejudicial grounds or because they correctly estimated Negroes to be relatively poor actuarial risks. Others wrote policies for Negroes but charged punitive premiums. As a consequence, early in this century a number of Negro life insurance companies were founded. In a highly technical enterprise requiring large amounts of capital, many failed, but by the 1940s there were more than 40 Negro insurance companies, and several were large and prosperous. The executives of the larger companies are still among the wealthiest Negroes in the country, and they represent the largest concentration of capital in financially sophisticated Negro hands.

However, most of the insurance in force on Negro lives is written by white-owned companies. It was estimated in the 1940s that one large white company had twice as much insurance on Negro lives as had all of the Negro companies combined (Pierce, p. 117). Since there is now little discrimination against Negroes by white insurance companies, the condition that gave the initial impetus to the Negro insurance business no longer exists. The larger size of the white companies gives them a competitive advantage, and therefore Negro companies are not likely to increase greatly their share of the insurance business.

In the publications field, Negro interests are not all served by the white press, and Negro publishing has been relatively prosperous. There are numerous Negro weekly newspapers, varying widely in quality and prosperity. Each of the larger Negro ghettos has a thriving weekly or daily that specializes in racial news and commentary but also gives space to matters of general interest. The *Chicago Defender* has a daily circulation of 31,000 in Chicago and a considerable weekly circulation outside the city. Other Negro newspapers with large circulations outside their home cities include the *Pittsburgh Courier,* printed in twelve editions with a total circulation of 77,000; the *Afro-American* (Baltimore), 31,000; and the *Journal and Guide* (Norfolk), 31,000. The most successful Negro magazine publisher is the Johnson Publishing Company of Chicago, publisher of *Ebony,* circulation 720,000; *Tan,* 126,000; *Jet,* 335,000; and the *Negro Digest. Ebony,* a picture magazine with a format similar to *Life,* is the most popular Negro magazine. Its circulation in 1963 was not far below that of *Esquire* and well above that of the *New Yorker*. Three monthly magazines are published in Fort Worth, Texas: *Bronze Thrills,* circulation 94,000; *Jive,* 91,000; and *Sepia,* 67,000 (Circulation figures from McAllister). Demand for specialized Negro periodicals will long continue, and their circulation will increase as the size, prosperity, and education of the Negro population increase. As the Negro market becomes more important, advertisers are turning increasingly to Negro periodicals, but competition will increase from publications of general circulation that have a growing awareness of the Negro consumer and his interests. Negro publishers have a brighter future than most other Negro businessmen, although it is uncertain whether they can maintain their independence in the face of the trend toward coalition and gigantism in the publishing business.

Decreases in racial segregation and discrimination are likely to hurt more than help Negro businessmen. If Negroes could more easily get credit and rent choice business locations and if whites would patronize their establishments, Negro business would be benefited, but most instances of reduced discrimination are detrimental to Negro business. Desegregation of white restaurants and other service establishments places Negro businessmen in direct competition with more efficient white enterprises. The immediate consequences of such desegregation have not been great, since most Negroes continue to patronize service establishments catering to Negroes and residential segregation with its concentrated Negro market gives local merchants some advantage over outside competition. But the long-run consequences may be more important. The breakup of ghettos and residential dispersion of Negroes might put many Negro establishments out of business, though in fact the current trend is not in this direction. Even Negro publications are dependent on race issues and distinctive Negro interests that are kept alive by segregation and discrimination. Undoubtedly, fuller integration of Negroes into the mainstream of

American life will restrict opportunities for Negro advancement in the segregated part of the economy.

Most future business opportunities for Negroes (as for whites) will be as employees of large firms, rather than as independent entrepreneurs, and in a biracial economy, rather than in a separate economy. What then are trends for Negro opportunities in the biracial economy? In the 1950s, they did not increase as rapidly as opportunities declined in the separate economy. Salaried male Negro managers increased by only about 3,500 from 1950 to 1960, or by about 20 percent, while self-employed Negro businessmen decreased by more than 10,000. In contrast, salaried male white managers increased by more than 40 percent. Only a small proportion of Negro managers were employed by Negro companies, and the number of these managers probably changed little during the 1950s. The overall increase in Negro managers was due in part to the hiring of Negroes to manage white-owned establishments in Negro neighborhoods. The number of Negroes in managerial positions in large corporations is likely to remain small for some time.

The founding of small businesses was until recently the primary means for manual workers in the United States to advance into middle-class occupations (Lipset and Bendix, pp. 172–178). With the decline of small business, this channel of occupational advancement is becoming restricted— one of the several trends that are widening the chasm between the opportunities of highly educated workers and others. This widening of the chasm affects Negroes as a whole much more than it affects whites, because a much larger percentage of Negroes are on the wrong side of the chasm. Opportunities for poorly educated Negroes to take the business route to middle-class status were never great, but now they are insignificant. As already emphasized, the chief avenues for advancement now open to Negroes are formal education and specialized vocational training for expanding lines of work.

The new Negro in the United States, like the new white, is an employee, not an entrepreneur. The employee status is a new condition for many whites, but few Negroes have ever been self-employed, except as tenant farmers. Therefore, the transition to an employee society may cause less strain for Negroes than for whites.

The Professions

The situation of Negro professional and semiprofessional workers is similar to that of Negro businessmen, since most serve other Negroes as entrepreneurs or employees of Negro institutions. Self-employed professionals suffer from many of the same handicaps as Negro businessmen. Usually they attract only a Negro clientele, and they must compete against whites for that. And most of their clients have limited ability to pay. Because of these and other handicaps, the representation of Negroes in the independent professions, such as medicine, dentistry, and law, was far less than the expected proportion in 1960 (see Table 5, p. 112). And in each of these there was a wide gap in earnings between whites and nonwhites (see Table 6, p. 114).

However, Negroes have been more successful in professional and technical work than in business, and Negro professionals have better prospects than Negro businessmen. In 1960, there were almost twice as many Negro male professional and technical workers as businessmen and managers, whereas the number of whites in these categories was about equal. Professional and technical workers were on the whole the most prosperous segment of the nonwhite population in 1959, ranking above salaried managers and far above self-employed businessmen. In contrast, among whites, salaried managers were on the average more prosperous than professional and technical workers.

The greater success of Negro professional and technical workers than of Negro businessmen is due to several factors. Perhaps almost a third of all Negro male professional and technical workers are now employed in the biracial economy, and this segment is increasing fairly rapidly. Well-qualified engineers, natural scientists, draftsmen, technicians, and similar workers face less discrimination now, because the demand for such workers exceeds the supply and companies cannot afford to discriminate. Around 60 percent of all Negro male professional and technical workers are employed by Negro institutions where they are protected from competition from whites. This 60 percent includes clergymen and most teachers and college professors. Less than 10 percent of Negro male professional and technical workers are self-employed, and even without institutional protection, they fare better than Negro businessmen. Because the practice of medicine and dentistry among poor Negroes is not very lucrative, there is little competition from whites for this practice. Custom in the South prescribes that different dental equipment must be used for Negroes and whites, and many white dentists do not buy the extra equipment needed for a Negro practice. However, the great majority of Southern Negroes receive little or no dental service from anyone, and therefore the number of Negro dentists relative to the size of the Negro population is smaller in the South than in the North.

The relative number of other Negro professional and technical workers also varies by region. Because of separate educational institutions, there are more Negro teachers and college professors, for example, per 10,000 Negro population in the South than elsewhere (see Table 11). However, the great majority of Negro professionals involved in the biracial economy live in regions other than the South, as do relatively more independent professionals. In all regions, the relative number of Negro teachers and social workers increased sharply during the 1950s, but Negro physicians and surgeons per 10,000 Negro population *declined* from 1950 to 1960, and the number of dentists and lawyers increased only slightly.

At first glance, it may seem surprising that Negroes have not entered the independent professions more rapidly. Negroes now have greater ability to pay for medical and other

TABLE 11. NUMBER OF EMPLOYED NEGRO WORKERS IN SELECTED PROFESSIONS PER 10,000 NEGRO POPULATION, BY REGION AND SEX, UNITED STATES, 1950 AND 1960

	U.S.		Northeast		North Central		South		West	
	1950	1960	1950	1960	1950	1960	1950	1960	1950	1960
Male:										
Physicians and surgeons	2.5	2.2	3.8	3.6	4.5	3.6	1.8	1.3	2.7	3.5
Dentists	1.0	1.1	2.1	1.8	1.5	1.2	0.7	0.8	1.2	1.3
Lawyers and judges	0.9	1.1	1.7	1.6	2.5	2.1	0.4	0.5	1.4	1.9
College professors[a]	1.7	1.9	0.5	0.8	0.8	1.0	2.2	2.5	0.4	0.5
Teachers[b]	12.5	16.4	4.2	9.0	7.4	10.8	15.7	20.5	3.9	11.1
Musicians and music teachers	3.7	3.0	9.2	4.8	5.8	3.3	1.7	2.2	11.1	6.3
Clergymen	12.1	7.4	10.1	5.5	11.2	6.2	12.5	8.3	13.8	6.7
Social workers	1.4	3.0	3.5	6.7	2.8	4.1	0.5	1.2	3.8	7.5
Pharmacists	0.8	1.0	1.3	1.0	1.5	1.5	0.4	0.4	1.5	1.3
Female:										
Teachers[b]	45.1	52.9	15.7	27.0	23.3	34.2	57.2	67.6	17.5	30.9

SOURCE: Computed from data from the 1950 and 1960 censuses of U.S. population.

[a] Excludes college professors who are enumerated in the census reports under their field of specialization. For instance, the chemist who is also a college professor is listed as a chemist and not as a college professor.

[b] Excludes music and art teachers.

professional services, and discrimination in medical, dental, and law schools outside the Deep South is no longer an important barrier. On the contrary, it is reported that in 1956 it would have been possible to have placed at least 200 more Negroes in predominantly white medical schools if qualified applicants could have been found (Reitzes, pp. 8–9). As late as 1947 there were not enough internships and residencies for Negro physicians, but by 1956 the shortage had been eliminated (McLean, pp. xxv–xxvi). Negro lawyers are now more likely to be treated fairly by the courts and should be able to compete more effectively against whites; civil rights litigation has itself provided work for many Negro lawyers.

One would expect these changes to lead to a sharp increase in independent Negro professionals, but it had not occurred by 1960. Given the generally poor quality of Negro education at the precollege and undergraduate levels, relatively few Negroes are qualified to enroll in professional schools. According to one study in the mid-1950s, only about 20 percent of the medical school applicants from Negro colleges were accepted (Reitzes, p. 10). In contrast, about 55 percent of all applicants to medical school were accepted. Although Negroes are now more prosperous, the cost of professional training has grown, and the proportion who can afford a professional education probably has not increased very much.

Studies of occupational change among whites are instructive when one seeks to understand the apparent lag in the number of Negro professionals. It is known that many white professionals come from prosperous business families, a common pattern of progression from generation to generation being from manual work to business to the professions (Rogoff; National Opinion Research Center). The direct jump from manual work to the professions in one generation is too difficult for most Negroes or whites. The lack of a prosperous Negro business class—and a missing generational bridge—retards Negro entry into professional work. More frequently clerical work has been the springboard from which Negroes have entered the professions (Edwards, p.

60), and the big increase in Negro clerical workers during the past 25 years may beget a big increase in professionals in the next generation.

Since there are more opportunities for Negroes to enter other well-paying occupations, a smaller percentage who have the financial and academic qualifications are entering professional schools. At one time, independent Negro professionals were much better off than Negroes in most other occupations, and many ambitious Negro youths aspired to be doctors or dentists. Now, however, they can enter many other occupations that require shorter formal preparation and offer earnings almost as high. For instance, in 1959 the median earnings of nonwhite physicians and surgeons were lower than the median earnings of nonwhite engineers and were only slightly higher than the median earnings of nonwhite accountants and auditors, electrical and electronics technicians, officials and administrators in public administration, designers and draftsmen, and teachers. The median earnings of nonwhite physicians and surgeons were only 40 percent higher than those of nonwhite male clerical and kindred workers—a rather small difference in view of the prolonged and expensive training of doctors. (In contrast, the median earnings of white physicians and surgeons were about 300 percent higher than those of white male clerical and kindred workers.) Thus, the relatively small financial returns from the professions may depress Negro enrollment in professional schools.

The number of Negro physicians may also be kept low because certain changes in the nature of medical practice and organization are working to the detriment of the Negro doctor (Hughes, p. 886). The growth of public health services and of Negro membership in group insurance schemes is tending to draw patients away from Negro doctors. Furthermore, medical practice is increasingly dependent upon access to the larger hospitals and clinics, where the capital goods and auxiliary personnel of medicine are concentrated. Negro physicians do not yet have adequate access to these facilities.

Desegregation of schools has tended to lessen opportunities for Negro teachers. Where schools are desegregated, Negro teachers encounter direct and difficult competition from whites. Even if there is no discrimination in teacher selection, Negroes are likely to fare poorly in the competition because they are not so well qualified on the average as whites. (The qualifications gap weighs heaviest in Southern and Border states where many Negro teachers are graduates of poor Negro colleges.) When schools are desegregated, wasteful duplication is often eliminated, and teaching staffs are reduced, and it is the less qualified and less influential Negro teachers who are more likely to be dismissed. For example, in three states where a significant number of schools were desegregated during the 1950s—West Virginia, Kentucky, and Oklahoma—the number of Negro teachers declined. In Kentucky and Oklahoma, the number of Negro teachers per 10,000 Negro population was lower in 1960 than in 1950 (see Table 12). Negroes also lost teaching jobs in some localities in Missouri and Texas, although increases in other parts of these states more than offset the losses (*South-*

TABLE 12. NUMBER OF NEGRO TEACHERS (BOTH SEXES) PER 10,000 NEGRO POPULATION, IN THE BORDER STATES AND DISTRICT OF COLUMBIA, 1950 AND 1960

	1950	1960	Percent change
Missouri	62	65	+ 3.8
Oklahoma	113	83	—25.9
West Virginia	84	95	+12.8
District of Columbia	70	85	+21.3
Delaware	61	68	+11.7
Maryland	63	77	+23.3
Kentucky	68	61	—11.0
All Border states and District of Columbia	71	75	+ 5.6
United States	58	69	+20.5

SOURCE: Computed from data from the 1950 and 1960 censuses of U.S. population.

ern School News, May, 1964). Negro teachers may be hurt even more when desegregation becomes widespread in the Deep South, where since 1954 several states have repealed tenure laws, so that public school teachers can now be dismissed without cause.

During the 1950s the employment of Negro teachers increased more slowly in the Border region, where desegregation was widespread, than in the country as a whole (see Table 12). The number of Negro teachers per 10,000 Negro population rose by less than 6 percent in the Border region, compared with the rise of more than 20 percent in the country as a whole.

Thus far, desegregation has affected opportunities for Negro college professors less than it has opportunities for public school teachers. Although desegregation has proceeded somewhat more rapidly in colleges than in public schools, a large majority of Negro college students in Border and Southern states are still enrolled in predominantly Negro colleges, and the enrollment in these colleges has continued to rise. Predominantly white colleges have drained off only a few thousand out of a total Negro enrollment near 100,000 in these regions. A few Negro colleges will close as a consequence of desegregation, but many will draw substantial Negro enrollments for a long time and will eventually become biracial institutions. A number are already technically biracial, although they enroll only a few whites. Increasing opportunities for highly qualified Negro professors in predominantly white colleges may more than offset losses in Negro colleges. Furthermore, the acute shortage of qualified faculty members at Negro colleges has kept the demand for them at a high level. On the other hand, opportunities for poorly qualified Negro professors are undoubtedly fewer than they would have been without desegregation.

Lack of qualified personnel rather than lack of opportunity accounts for the limited increase in Negro college professors during recent years. And the lack of qualified personnel results mainly from the generally poor quality of

Negro education and inadequate finances for the long period of graduate training. Furthermore, the opening of technical and clerical jobs in government and industry is deflecting Negroes away from graduate school. More fellowships, assistantships, and other financial assistance for graduate training will probably attract more Negroes to college teaching, but the increase will not be great until improvements in education in the public schools and at the undergraduate level produce a larger number of Negroes capable of benefiting from graduate training.

Entertainers and Athletes

For several decades a few Negroes in show business and professional sports have achieved fame and fortune before audiences of whites as well as Negroes. Only with the recent ascendancy of protest leaders have other Negroes gained as much prominence. Entertainers and athletes still constitute a large proportion of high-income Negroes. Millions of whites who would not patronize a Negro-owned store or go to a Negro doctor or lawyer are devoted fans of such Negro celebrities as Louis Armstrong, Willie Mays, and Sidney Poitier, the 1963 Oscar acting-award winner.

Low educational level does not so seriously impede advancement in these fields since neither athletics nor many forms of popular entertainment require much formal education. Popularization of music that originated with Negroes has given Negro musicians a special advantage.

Negro entertainers with local reputations perform for white and mixed audiences, even in the South. The Southern white night club patron accepts a Negro entertainer as readily as a Negro waiter. Both are "service" workers performing roles traditionally defined as appropriate for Negroes, but the types of performance considered appropriate are becoming less restricted. The Negro jazz musician has long been taken for granted in the South, but the Negro singer of romantic songs has only recently gained acceptance there. The result is twofold: a broadening of Negro employment opportunities to include a wider range of skills and talent and at the same time increased competition from whites in types of entertainment, such as jazz, in which Negroes have had a large share. The popularity of Negro entertainers and dance bands has contributed to the increase in the number of Negro-owned night clubs that cater successfully to a mixed clientele in several cities, including a few in the South.

Even though Negroes are far less handicapped in the biracial economy in entertainment and athletics than in most occupations, representation in these fields is less than proportional. Skills that require long and expensive periods of training, such as classical music, operatic singing, and serious drama, understandably have recruited fewer Negroes than the more popular art forms. Negro actresses and actors have performed on Broadway and in movies, but until recently they were usually restricted to stereotyped roles. Much the same situation obtained in television. Before 1963, few Negroes were cast except as racial stereotypes, but since then casting has broadened. Television commercials also have become increasingly "integrated."

Some of the Negro prominence in professional sports is directly related to poverty. Negroes have long had easy access to boxing, for example, which recruits most of its professionals from poorly educated and disadvantaged parts of the population to whom less hazardous avenues of financial gain are generally not accessible. Fifty years ago many boxers were low-status European immigrants, but during the past thirty years a disproportionate number have been Negroes and Latin Americans. Six of the last eight heavyweight champions were Negroes.

In the early years of boxing, Negro participation was complicated by racial issues, and race was exploited to stimulate public interest, although a Negro who was a dangerous contender for a championship sometimes found it difficult to get the opportunity he earned. Racial, religious, and national antagonisms were used for the sake of the gate, and an interracial championship fight generated tension that often spilled over into the streets. Jess Willard was a "White Hope" who finally won the crown from the Negro Jack Johnson, thereby re-establishing a kind of white supremacy. In recent years, the preoccupation of whites with the race-conflict aspects of boxing has declined, but the long list of champions is still a source of pride for Negroes.

In professional team sports, Negroes have gained entry more recently. Major league baseball was not opened to Negroes until 1947 when Jackie Robinson was moved from a minor league team to the Brooklyn Dodgers. Many other Negroes were soon recruited, and about a hundred now play in the major leagues. Professional football and basketball have had some Negro players for a number of years, but because these sports depend largely on colleges as training grounds, Negroes in the South have been handicapped: The Southeast Conference excludes Negroes from all athletic teams, and racial bars were not lowered in the Southwest Conference until the 1964 season. This is yet another instance, although a minor one, in which the policies of educational institutions affect Negro occupational status. There are still few Negro professionals in such nonteam sports as golf, tennis, and bowling.

Despite the publicity given to entertainers and professional athletes, neither show business nor sports is likely to be a major means of Negro economic advancement. Only a small percentage of Negroes are employed in these fields, and only a small percentage of these have more than modest incomes. However, Negro celebrities have had an important effect upon Negro morale and upon white attitudes toward Negroes. The celebrity is conspicuous proof that Negroes can rise above the stereotype and the dead level of poverty. He enhances Negro pride and whets the Negro appetite for success.

The image of success and its effects on the aspirations of young Negroes are not simple things. Success in athletics, associated as it often is with gambling and marginal criminality, is surrounded with an aura of luck and the "fix." The aspirations generated by the ideal of the sports hero may be wishes for the "fast buck," the good connection, the meteoric rise, not reward for steady effort, hard-won skill, and solid achievement. To the extent that the image of sports heroes encourages dreams of easy success, the result may be to reduce realistic application of Negro youth to education and conventional jobs. But if race pride inspires personal resolve and sustained effort, the consequences can be higher achievement in many fields.

The adulation of a Negro celebrity by white fans, especially younger ones, may result in more positive feelings towards Negroes in general. His money and popularity give him access to important whites, and he may exert his influence on behalf of race causes. Therefore, the increase in Negro celebrities during the past two or three decades may be of more importance than the numbers involved. However, a celebrity's opinions are often sought and quoted for reasons irrelevant to the issue under question. His comments are worth publicity because he is a public figure, not because he speaks with authority or knowledge on the subject of an interview. The publicized comments of Negro celebrities who have little education sometimes have a degrading effect on the public image of the Negro, but bizarre utterances of white celebrities are not generalized to the white population.

The Negro celebrity is expected to speak out on race issues, and action organizations strive to enlist him as a spokesman, or at least urge him publicly to declare his allegiance to the organization. Unless he is unusually vigilant, he will find words that he never uttered placed in his mouth by organization publicists or reporters.

Government Employment

Some of the best opportunities for Negro professional, technical, and clerical workers are in government employment—an expanding sector of the economy. As we have pointed out, Negro opportunities tend to be greatest in fields in which jobs are increasing most rapidly. Furthermore, civil service jobs are supposedly granted on the basis of examination scores and other objective criteria, and if the hiring personnel adhere to prescribed procedures, discrimination is reduced. The growing political influence of Negroes has been accompanied by declining discrimination in the federal government, in state and municipal governments in the North, West and, recently, in some Border and Southern states.

Negroes have been more than proportionally represented in federal employment since World War II. Whereas they comprised about 10 percent of the total labor force in 1962, they were 13 percent of all federal employees (Hope and Shelton, p. 370). Almost 5 percent of all employed Negroes were employed by the federal government. However, Negroes were only 9.1 percent of Classification Act (white-collar) employees. They were 18.6 percent of Wage Board (manual) employees, 15.1 percent of Postal Field Service employees, and 8.1 percent of other federal employees. In each category, they were concentrated in the lower grades. For instance, 18.2 percent of the Classification Act workers in grades GS-1 through 4 were Negro, but only 5.5 percent in grades GS-5 through 11 and 0.8 percent in grades GS-12 through 18 were Negro (Hope and Shelton, p. 369).* However, from 1961 to 1962, the first year of the Kennedy administration, Negro representation increased appreciably in the middle levels, partly as a result of the administration policy to upgrade Negroes where possible.

A scarcity of qualified people largely explains the small representation of Negroes in the higher grades, and appreciable upgrading must await improved qualifications or widespread reverse discrimination. However, discrimination and the failure of Negroes to apply for jobs because they think they would be discriminated against are important addi-

* The salary range for GS grades 1 through 4 is $3,385 through $5,830; for grades 5 through 11 it is $5,000 through $11,305; and for grades 12 through 18 it is $10,250 through $24,500.

tional reasons for low Negro representation in federal employment in the South. (In 1962, less than 8 percent of the federal employees in Texas, Mississippi, Florida, and Arkansas were Negro, whereas from 12 to 42 percent of the populations of these states are Negro.) Many Southern Negroes are rural, and rural Negroes may not know about or be qualified for government jobs. Even urban Negroes may be less likely to aspire to government employment in the South, because traditionally they have been excluded from such work. A Department of Labor official recently concluded, on the basis of discussions at eighteen Negro colleges, that Southern Negroes are reluctant to take civil service examinations, either because they do not know the procedure or because they believe that seeking white-collar government employment is futile (Mendelson, p. 91).

The federal civil service system in the South is administered by white Southerners, many of whom are prejudiced or wish to avoid the friction that results from breaching traditional mores. It is to be expected that administrators who want to discriminate will find ways to do so. The United States Commission on Civil Rights, created by Congress in 1957, found evidence of discrimination in the field establishments of federal agencies that have good records of hiring Negroes in Washington (Mendelson, pp. 81–82). The elimination of discrimination in federal employment in the South will require more than the enunciation of formal policies of nondiscrimination from Washington. The transfer of prejudiced administrators and rigorous field reviews of hiring would seem to be minimum conditions to any significant change.

Negroes have long been well represented in government employment in those Northern and Western states, cities, and counties that have large numbers of Negroes. Again, most are in manual and clerical work, and their small representation at higher levels results from both discrimination and a dearth of well-qualified Negroes. Southern and Border states, cities, and counties rarely employ Negroes except in low-level manual work, but cracks are appearing in this traditional pattern: in Texas, a few Negroes have been appointed to intermediate-level government posts, for example, assistant attorney general and assistant district attorneys in Dallas and Harris (Houston) counties. An increasing, but still small, number of Negroes are employed as craftsmen and clerical workers by the state and by local governments in Texas.

Although there appears to be less discrimination by government agencies than by private industry, only a small percent of Negroes can hope to find government work. Like all other work, it increasingly requires higher skills and therefore is not open to the poorly educated and unskilled. Removal of all remaining discrimination against Negroes in government employment, or even considerable reverse discrimination, would effect only a small closing of the occupational and income gaps in the total labor force. Closing of these gaps depends more upon removal of racial barriers in private employment, where most jobs are located, and, as we have repeatedly emphasized, an increase in the relative qualifications of Negroes.

8

Characteristics of the Negro
Population

Size and Distribution

In order to understand the condition and prospects of the Negro in the United States, the changing size, composition, and geographical distribution of the Negro population must be examined in some detail.

The number of Negroes has grown steadily from the first United States census in 1790 to the present, but during most of that period the white population increased more rapidly. Whereas Negroes were almost one-fifth of the total population in 1790, they were less than one-tenth in 1930. Until the decline of European immigration in the 1920s, many thousands of whites but few Negroes entered the country each decade, and the natural increase of whites was higher during much of that period. The Negro death rate was higher than the white death rate, but Negro and white birth rates probably differed little until around 1900. By the 1930s, however, white fertility was far below that of Negroes, the net immigration of whites was negligible, and consequently Negroes

157

started to increase slightly as a percentage of the total population, from 9.7 percent in 1930, to 9.8 in 1940, to 10.0 in 1950, to 10.5 in 1960. This increase probably will continue for some time, but Negroes are not likely to be much more than one-tenth of all Americans in the near future.

The recent small change in the relative size of the Negro American population has had no appreciable effect upon Negro status. However, the size of a minority population compared with the whole population and its relative size in specific localities do affect its chances for advancement. Were Negro Americans a much larger percentage of the population, white resistance to their advancement would perhaps be more severe, since whites would fear being displaced from jobs by Negroes. As it is, Negroes in the United States can now rise slowly in jobs and income without noticeably displacing whites. In fact, during a period such as the last two decades, when upper- and middle-level jobs are rapidly expanding and there is a general upward movement in the job market, Negroes can advance fairly rapidly without any downward displacement of whites (Glenn *d*, pp. 111–113).

On the other hand, a minority population can benefit in some ways from being relatively numerous. If they have the franchise, their political influence increases with their relative numbers. If Negroes in the United States were no more numerous than American Indians, for instance, Presidential candidates and other office seekers would have little concern for the Negro vote. Furthermore, a large minority, even though poor, has buying power that can be used as a potent weapon for gaining economic and political concessions.

The geographic distribution of a minority population also affects its status. Whereas Negro Americans make up about 10 percent of the total population, they have been concentrated in localities where they far exceeded the national percentage. White resistance was greater in these areas than it would have been if Negroes had been distributed more evenly. The redistribution of Negroes in recent decades probably has helped Negro advancement, over and above the direct influence of economic and job opportunities that prompted the redistribution.

During the decade following 1910, the great migration of Negroes from the rural South began with the push of a depression in Southern agriculture and the pull of new opportunities for industrial employment in the North. Probably the pull was the more important factor. Previously, new workers in the lower echelons of the industrial labor force were recruited largely from European immigrants. World War I reduced immigration and increased the demand for new workers, thus creating a labor vacuum into which thousands of Southern Negroes could move. The northward migration subsided during the depression of 1920–1921, resumed by 1924 when the heavy flow of European immigrants was permanently stopped, and subsided again during the Great Depression of 1929–1939. The Negro exodus from the South reached a new high during World War II and the period of postwar prosperity, but in this later migration large

TABLE 13. PERCENTAGE OF NEGRO AND OF TOTAL POPULATION IN EACH REGION, UNITED STATES, 1910–1960

	Northeast	North Central	South	West	Total
Negro					
1910	4.9	5.5	89.0	0.5	100.0
1920	6.5	7.6	85.2	0.8	100.0
1930	9.6	10.6	78.7	1.0	100.0
1940	10.6	11.0	77.0	1.3	100.0
1950	13.4	14.8	68.0	3.8	100.0
1960	16.0	18.3	59.9	5.8	100.0
1966	16.8	20.0	55.2	8.0	100.0
Total population					
1910	28.1	32.5	31.8	7.4	100.0
1920	28.1	32.2	31.3	8.4	100.0
1930	28.0	31.4	30.8	9.7	100.0
1940	27.3	30.5	31.6	10.5	100.0
1950	26.2	29.5	31.3	13.0	100.0
1960	24.9	28.8	30.7	15.6	100.0
1966	24.6	27.9	31.0	16.5	100.0

SOURCE: Computed from data from the 1910 through **1960** censuses of U.S. population and Current Population Reports, Series P-20.

numbers of Negroes joined the movement to the West.

The regional distributions of Negro and total U.S. populations from 1910 to 1966 are shown in Table 13 and the percentage of the population that was Negro in each region in the same period is shown in Figure 3. Clearly, problems associated with large numbers of Negroes are no longer restricted to the South. All heavily industrialized states now have sizable Negro populations, and 45 percent of all Negroes live outside of the South.

The trend for the Negro distribution through the country to resemble that of whites can be indicated by a measure called the "index of dissimilarity," which shows the percentage of Negroes who would have to change their state of residence in order for the Negro and white distributions to be the same. Therefore, the lower the index value, the closer the distribution of Negroes resembles that of whites. This value in the United States, excluding Alaska and Hawaii, declined from 50 for 1940, to 41 for 1950, to 34 for 1960. These figures are based only on *interstate* differences, and Negroes and whites are very differently distributed among localities within some states. For instance, the proportion of Negroes in Texas is not far above the national figure, but in some areas of East Texas, the proportion of Negroes is around one-half. Likewise, Negroes comprise about one-tenth of the population of Illinois but are almost one-quarter of the population of Chicago.

One important aspect of the geographical redistribution of Negroes is a reduction in the number of localities in the South in which Negroes outnumber whites. In 1910, there were 264 counties in 12 Southern and Border states with populations 50 percent or more Negro; by 1960, the number of such counties had declined to 123. In 1910, nearly 40 percent of all Negroes lived in predominantly Negro counties in these states, whereas by 1960 only 7 percent did so. This change undoubtedly aided Negro advance in the South, since there is evidence that discrimination is greater and that

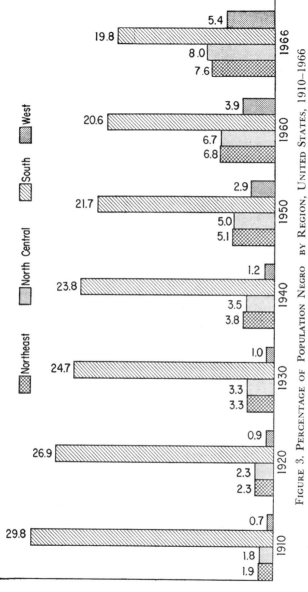

FIGURE 3. PERCENTAGE OF POPULATION NEGRO BY REGION, UNITED STATES, 1910–1966

SOURCE: Computed from data from the 1910 through 1960 censuses of U.S. population and Current Population Reports, Series P-20.

Negro status on the average is lower in Southern localities with large proportions of Negroes. For instance, white resistance to Negro voting is related to the relative size of the Negro population (Heer, pp. 592–598). Where Negroes are relatively few and can be outvoted, whites do not fear the Negro franchise. Also, the average Negro income is lower where Negroes are a larger percentage of the population (Glenn *e*). Throughout the South, most Negroes are restricted to a narrow range of occupations and, the more Negroes there are to compete for the "Negro jobs," the lower Negro wages will be. For these reasons, the decrease in the percentage of Negro population in the South has contributed to Negro economic, political, and educational gains in that region.

At the same time, the Negro percentage of the population has increased sharply in many localities in the North and West. The increases from 1950 to 1960 in several of the larger metropolitan areas are shown in Table 14. Prejudice and discrimination may be influenced outside the South as well as in the South by the relative size of the Negro population, but the evidence is not so convincing. There is some indication that anti-Negro sentiments have increased as the Negro population has grown in Northern and Western cities, but the most overt and aggressive kinds of discrimination have not increased correspondingly. In part, this is due to anti discrimination legislation passed by legislatures of states with growing Negro electorates.

As thousands of Negroes moved from the rural areas of the South to Northern and Western cities, thousands more moved to Southern cities. Urbanization started later with Negroes than with whites, but Negroes are now slightly more urban. In 1910, nearly 50 percent of whites lived in cities compared with just over 25 percent of Negroes. By 1960, 73 percent of Negroes and 70 percent of whites were urban. Negro urbanization, like many other changes in the Negroes' situation, was accelerated by World War II. The percent of urban Negroes jumped from 49 in 1940 to 62 in 1950, while

TABLE 14. PERCENTAGE OF THE POPULATION NEGRO IN
SELECTED METROPOLITAN AREAS, 1950 AND 1960[a]

	1950	1960
Baltimore	19.8	21.9
Boston	2.2	3.0
Chicago	10.7	14.4
Cincinnati	10.5	12.0
Cleveland	10.4	14.9
Detroit	11.9	14.9
Los Angeles-Long Beach	5.0	6.9
New York	8.1	10.5
Philadelphia	13.1	15.5
Pittsburgh	6.2	6.7
San Francisco-Oakland	6.6	8.6
St. Louis	12.8	14.3
Washington, D.C.	23.1	24.3

SOURCE: Computed from data from the 1950 and 1960 censuses of U.S. population.

[a] The 1950 data are for census units designated "Standard Metropolitan Areas." The 1960 data for New York and Chicago are for "Standard Consolidated Areas," and the other data are for "Standard Metropolitan Statistical Areas." In each case, the 1950 and 1960 boundaries are the same, or are very similar.

the percent of urban whites went from 58 to 64. Not only are Negroes now more urban than whites, they are more highly concentrated in large metropolitan areas. Thirty percent of urban Negroes compared with 26 percent of urban whites lived in the twelve largest metropolitan areas in 1960. Within the metropolitan areas, Negroes are concentrated in the central cities whereas a large percentage of whites lives in the suburbs. In the twelve most populous metropolitan areas in 1960, 55 percent of the whites lived outside the central cities, compared with only 19 percent of the Negroes.

Both the geographical redistribution and the urbanization of Negroes have had important effects on the recent change in the posture of Negroes. Movement from the rural South broke the "cake of custom" and made Negroes receptive to further change. In the semifeudal society of the rural South, there were few influences to upset traditional relations, and authority, backed by the threat of physical harm, kept the Negro in his socially defined place. As already mentioned, even the Negro leaders—the ministers—did not challenge the legitimacy of white domination. Many Negroes were never exposed to the idea that they could be equal to whites, and they accepted their inferior status as an unchangeable aspect of the nature of things. This does not mean that they were contented, as the sentimental view of the Old South would have it. Rather, they were resigned to their condition and they adapted to it as best they could. As discussed in Chapter 1, escape from grim reality through other-worldly religion was a characteristic means of adaptation.

When Negroes moved to the Northern cities, however, they learned that aspects of race relations they had hitherto accepted as certain and unchangeable were not in evidence. For the first time, many were exposed to the ideal of racial equality, and they came to view the position of Negroes vis-à-vis whites as susceptible of change. Resignation was tentatively replaced by qualified optimism, and race discrimination was no longer considered a condition permanently to be endured. The change was not so great for those who migrated to Southern cities, but they too were often exposed to heterodox ideas and became imbued with the characteristic urban secularism and rationality that so often disrupt traditional social relations. This was especially true of middle-class Negroes, who emerged in significant numbers in the urban South as well as in the North.

The Negro movement out of the rural South and to the cities affected those who stayed behind as well as the migrants. Visits and letters from friends and relatives who had migrated exposed rural Southern Negroes to new ideas and awakened them to the possibility of a different way of life. Although rural Negroes remain the most accommodative and complacent segment of the Negro population, many now hope for, and perhaps are willing to take action to bring about, basic changes in their status.

With the increase in the number of Negroes in cities and

in regions where whites openly espouse the ideal of racial equality, it was inevitable that Negro pressure for elimination of racial discrimination would increase. It did not seem inevitable, however, that this increased pressure would bring about the surge of Negro protest activity of 1963. The urbanization and geographical redistribution of Negroes were not new; they had been proceeding rapidly for many years. But the cumulative effects of these trends combined with other long-range trends to produce the "Revolt of '63."

Mortality and Fertility

Life itself is given in smaller measure to Negroes. In 1920, a white person at birth could look forward to 55 years of life, a Negro to only 45. Put another way, the life expectancy of nonwhites at birth was 83 percent that of whites (see Table 15). Since 1920, life expectancy of both whites and nonwhites has improved, but the increase has been greater for nonwhites. By 1960, the life expectancy of nonwhites was 90 percent that of whites, or slightly lower than that of whites twenty years earlier. Since 1900 or perhaps earlier, death rates for both races have followed a downward course, but the nonwhite rate has lagged by two to three decades. This lag is exemplified in mortality under one year of age (see Fig. 4). Infant mortality for nonwhites in 1960 was identical to the white rate in 1940; there was a similar pattern at most other age levels.

The difference between Negroes and whites in life expectancy results primarily from far-reaching differences in education, income, and occupation and associated differences in living conditions, occupational hazards, and knowledge of and access to medical facilities.* In other words, it is pri-

---

* It is unlikely that any of the Negro-white difference in life expectancy is due to hereditary factors. The greater incidence among Negroes of several diseases, including tuberculosis and other respiratory diseases, can be accounted for by nutritional and other environmental factors. However, at least one hereditary disorder, sickle-cell anemia, is more common among Negroes, but some other hereditary blood diseases are more frequent among whites (Pettigrew and Pettigrew, pp. 327–328).

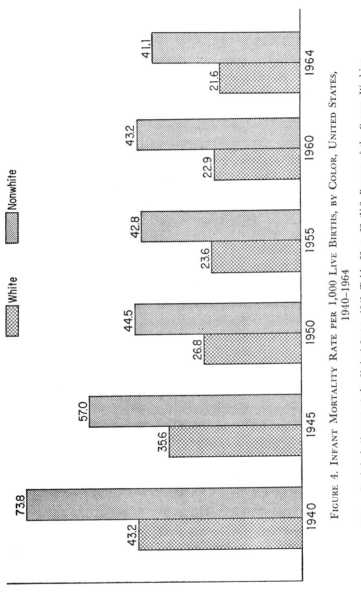

FIGURE 4. INFANT MORTALITY RATE PER 1,000 LIVE BIRTHS, BY COLOR, UNITED STATES, 1940–1964

SOURCE: *Statistical Abstract of the United States, 1963*, Table 66, p. 62 (U.S. Bureau of the Census, Washington, D.C.). Data for 1964 supplied by Department of Health, Education and Welfare.

TABLE 15. EXPECTATION OF LIFE AT BIRTH, IN YEARS, BY COLOR AND SEX, UNITED STATES, 1920–1964

Year	White	Nonwhite	Ratio of non-white to white
Both sexes			
1920	54.9	45.3	.83
1930	61.4	48.1	.78
1940	64.2	53.1	.83
1950	69.1	60.8	.88
1960	70.6	63.6	.90
1964	71.0	64.1	.90
Males			
1920	54.4	45.5	.84
1930	59.7	47.3	.79
1940	62.1	51.5	.83
1950	66.5	59.1	.89
1960	67.4	61.1	.91
1964	67.7	61.1	.90
Females			
1920	55.6	45.2	.81
1930	63.5	49.2	.77
1940	66.6	54.9	.82
1950	72.2	62.9	.87
1960	74.1	66.3	.89
1964	74.6	67.2	.90

SOURCE: *Statistical Abstract of the United States: 1963,* Table 63, p. 59. Data for 1964 supplied by Department of Health, Education and Welfare.

marily related to social class rather than to race. A similar difference has been found for whites (Guralnick).

However, Negroes are subjected to some unique health hazards Only segregated hospital facilities are available in many Southern localities, and the Negro facilities are almost invariably inferior. Not all white doctors give Negro patients the same care and attention they give whites, and Negro doctors on the average are not very well trained. Furthermore, overcrowding, a result of housing discrimination and poverty, is adverse to health. Consequently, some difference in life expectancy and incidence of disease is likely to remain as long as Negroes are generally disadvantaged.

The closing of the longevity gap between Negroes and whites can be affected by other factors besides convergence in education, income, and occupation. For example, white mortality has declined to a level below which further reduction will be slow and largely dependent upon breakthroughs in the prevention and treatment of such disorders as cancer and heart disease. Since a larger percentage of Negro deaths could be prevented through application of presently available preventive and therapeutic measures, Negro mortality is likely to continue to decline after white mortality becomes virtually stable. Absolute increases in Negro status and extension of public health and welfare services should bring about further convergence of Negro and white life expectancy—but no appreciable convergence occurred from 1955 to 1960.

The relatively poor health of Negroes tends to perpetuate the very conditions that cause it. Poor health reduces work efficiency and contributes to high job absenteeism. Premature death of many Negro parents exacerbates problems of Negro dependency, considerable anyway because of high rates of illegitimacy, divorce, and separation in the Negro lower class. Many young Negroes must drop out of school or college because of the death or disability of parents, and they in turn become more susceptible to chronic disease and premature death.

As noted at the beginning of this chapter, the Negro population is increasing more rapidly than the white population, in spite of higher Negro mortality, since Negro fertility is higher than white fertility, and the difference is persisting. Live birth rates per 1,000 population for whites and for nonwhites from 1920 through 1962 are shown in Figure 5. Both the percentage difference and the absolute difference between white and nonwhite birth rates were greater in 1962 than in 1920. The absolute difference has remained about 10 points, except during the 1930s and early 1940s, when it was well below 10 points. A more refined measure is the number of

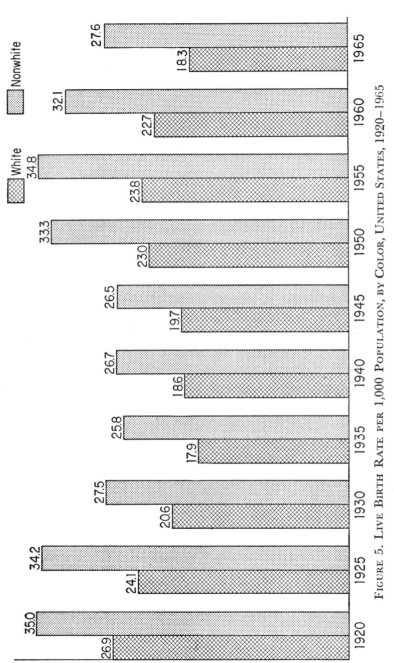

FIGURE 5. LIVE BIRTH RATE PER 1,000 POPULATION, BY COLOR, UNITED STATES, 1920–1965

SOURCE: *Statistical Abstract of the United States, 1963*, Table 50, p. 52 (U.S. Bureau of the Census, Washington, D.C.). Data for 1965 from Department of Health, Education and Welfare.

children ever born per 1,000 women, 15 through 44 years old. According to this measure, given in Table 16, the ratio of nonwhite to white fertility did converge until 1950, after which there was a minor divergence as nonwhite fertility increased faster than white fertility.

TABLE 16. NUMBER OF CHILDREN EVER BORN PER 1,000 WOMEN, 15 THROUGH 44 YEARS OLD, BY COLOR, CONTERMINOUS UNITED STATES, 1910, 1940, 1950, AND 1960

Year	White	Nonwhite	Ratio of non-white to white
1910	1,662	2,091	1.26
1940	1,186	1,451	1.22
1950	1,372	1,572	1.15
1960	1,712	2,003	1.17

SOURCE: *U.S. Census of Population: 1960*, Final Report PC(1)-1C; *United States Summary*, Table 81 (U.S. Bureau of the Census, Washington, D.C.).

The higher birth rate among nonwhites is not attributable to a greater biological capacity of Negroes. Most women, Negro or white, could bear far more children than they do. The difference in fertility can be explained mainly by differences in education, income, and occupation. On the average, educated women, and wives of well-educated husbands, have fewer children than do couples with less education. Wives of white-collar workers on the average have fewer children than wives of manual workers, and middle-income families average fewer children than low-income families. Since few Negroes are highly educated and most are manual workers with low incomes, one would expect their fertility to be relatively high, as it is. Well-educated Negroes in white-collar occupations with good incomes are, if anything, less fertile than whites of comparable status.

Because there has been some convergence of Negro and white educational, occupational, and economic characteristics, over the long run one would expect a corresponding convergence in fertility. The lack of such a trend since 1950 may be caused by improvement in prenatal and natal care and a decline in the rate of Negro miscarriages or stillbirths. There was a marked decrease in childlessness among urban nonwhite women after 1940 (Kiser, pp. 196–197). The earlier high rate of childlessness was in part due to family disorganization and widespread venereal infection among recent migrants from rural areas. Public health measures reduced venereal disease and helped to increase Negro fertility, both absolutely and relative to white fertility. Finally, some of the rise in the Negro birth rate may be more apparent than real— a consequence of more nearly complete recording of births. Urban births are more likely to be fully recorded than rural births, and more Negroes are now urban. Also, the increased importance of Negroes in the eyes of government officials has led to more nearly complete enumeration of Negroes in censuses and in birth and death records.

The continued higher fertility of Negroes does not mean that Negroes will soon become a much larger percentage of the total population and that race relations will thereby be appreciably affected. But the higher Negro fertility is important for another reason: a large number of children is a great burden to the low-income family. Negro families average only about 50 percent the income of white families, but their average number of children is about 30 percent more. High fertility not only aggravates the present poverty of Negroes; it also reduces the chances of advancement of the children. Sociological research on social mobility gives ample evidence that children from small families, regardless of race, stand better chances of occupational, economic, and educational advancement than do children in large families (Lipset and Bendix, pp. 238–243). Furthermore, high Negro fertility makes for overcrowding of schools in predominantly Negro areas and lessens the chances that Negro children, including those from small families, will be well educated. Lowered fertility would benefit Negroes in several ways, but any appreciable reduction in Negro fertility probably depends on the very types of advancement—especially educational—that such a reduction would help promote.

9

Perspective and Prospects

Forces behind the Transformation

An improvement in education, occupation, and economic condition has marked the transformation of the Negro American, and in these respects the gap between Negroes and whites has been considerably reduced in the past half century. Once predominantly a Southern agricultural population, Negroes are now predominantly urban, highly concentrated in the largest metropolitan areas, 40 percent living outside the South. Negroes now live longer and healthier lives, although still not so long nor healthy as whites. Negro-white cultural differences have diminished. All these are changes of great significance, and they have important bearings on the future. But the most pronounced and striking aspect of the transformation has been a sharp rise in Negro aspirations, a shift from accommodation and quiet resignation to an urgent demand and struggle for equality. In this chapter, we are concerned with the forces behind this change, the most recent and conspicuous aspects of which are often called the Negro "revolt."

Throughout the book, we refer to an increase in Negro discontent and restiveness, but there is no evidence that Negroes have become more acutely unhappy. Rather there have been increased *expressions* of discontent and a focusing of Negro dissatisfaction upon discrimination and segregation. Discontent has turned outward rather than inward, and people have been spurred to action. At least in the upper and middle levels of Negro society, there is an optimism in discontent, an anticipation of a better future. In recent years, action has often achieved results. The achievements mitigate dissatisfaction, but they do not lead to quiescence. Instead, the consequence of action is more action, strengthened by growing experience, confidence, and conviction.

The optimism that tempers discontent occurs even at rather low levels in Negro society, but it is neither so common nor so strong there. Almost two-thirds of the Negroes polled in a 1954 survey said they believed that life would be better in the next few years. A larger percentage of highly educated than of poorly educated Negroes gave this response, but over half of those with only a grammar school education were optimistic. Although Negro progress during the following few years was slow, polls in 1959 and in 1963 showed that a majority of Negroes were still optimistic (Pettigrew *b*, p. 185).

However, among some unskilled, poorly educated Negroes there was reason for an increase in discontent untempered by optimism. In the intervening years, their relative economic standing declined, and in some cases, so did their absolute economic condition. For instance, nonwhite males 25 years old or older with no formal education (and there were still 316,000 in 1960) had a median income, in constant dollars, 3 percent smaller in 1959 than in 1949. Furthermore, from 1949 to 1959 the median income of uneducated nonwhite males fell from 32 percent to 19 percent of the median income of college-educated nonwhites and from 22 percent to 13 percent of the median income of college-educated whites.*

---

* Nonwhite males with no formal schooling were on the average rather old, and their decreased median income could be accounted for by a larger percentage retired or disabled in 1959. The sharp decline in their relative income, however, is not entirely explainable in that way. The median income

Those at the bottom of Negro society have not shared in the general prosperity of postwar America nor have they shared in the general Negro advancement. Their discontent grows primarily out of decreased opportunities, not increased aspirations. As the demand for unskilled, uneducated workers declines, their plight is likely to become worse; if they are optimistic, their hopefulness is unrealistic.

Negro discontent is not the same thing among the different class levels; it differs in its sources and in its consequences. Whereas justifiably optimistic discontent leads to a strongly felt but usually prudent attack upon discrimination and segregation, the less hopeful discontent is likely to lead to hostility, predatory activities, and renunciation of the goal of integration. If technological unemployment becomes more prevalent at higher skill levels, more Negroes are likely to become discontented without sustaining optimism.

Let us now review the forces that have raised Negro aspirations, that have motivated action, and that have released expressions of discontent. We do not claim that our treatment is exhaustive, but we do touch upon the more important influences that have transformed American race relations during the past few decades and especially during the past few years. Earlier chapters indicate that the various forces are not independent of one another. In this discussion, we attempt to underscore the interrelations.

A basic factor in the change in race relations was the geographical redistribution of Negroes. Movement of Negroes to Northern cities made them more receptive to change, and many constraints upon their action to improve their status were removed. Whereas extra legal coercion, the law, the police, and courts in the South combined to keep the Negro in the place defined by law and custom, he found that the law in the North was often on his side. Because the intimate, paternalistic relations between Negroes and their employers

---

of nonwhite males with only a few years of education, who were not so old on the average, also declined sharply compared with that of better educated nonwhites.

were not common in the North, race relations were less personal, and Negroes were rarely deterred from protest activity by devotion to or dependence upon white employers. Through visits and letters to friends and relatives, the effects of the migration to the North upon Negro attitudes flowed back to the South.

The full impact of Northern life upon Negro ambitions did not come until the second and third generations. Although some migrants became disillusioned with the North, finding it less than the Promised Land they had expected, apparently most experienced some relief from the more direct and humiliating forms of white domination. Although Negroes were at the bottom of the Northern economy, most of them enjoyed higher incomes and better living conditions than they had in the South. Since they measured their situation against their Southern past, they were fairly well satisfied. In contrast, their children and grandchildren with little or no experience in the South measure their situation against the standard of equality and the conditions of Northern whites (Bindman *b*, pp. 114–115). The Negro reared in the North is more sensitive to the subtler forms of discrimination practiced there. He does not consider his lot to be relatively good, because he has not known worse. For the first time, there are substantial numbers of adult and adolescent Negroes born in the North and West, and they are probably more active in the civil rights movement than migrants from the South.

As Negroes moved out of the rural South, their capabilities for concerted action increased. In the cities, they grew more sophisticated in the use of their growing economic and political power. Negroes who participated in the labor movement adapted to the struggle for Negro rights techniques learned from organized labor.* Their purchasing power increased, and when they developed enough unity and organization to

---

* Bindman found that all of the Negro leaders in an Illinois protest movement had worked in industrial plants and come into contact with the AFL-CIO, and two of them had been AFL-CIO stewards (Bindman *b*, p. 18).

use their dollars for racial objectives, businessmen who catered to them could no longer ignore their feelings and demands. Concentration of Negroes in the populous states greatly enhanced Negro political power, and no Presidential candidate (nor a candidate for office in the large Northern and Western states) can now afford to ignore Negro demands. The Presidential election of 1960 illustrates the importance of the Negro vote in a close election when the white vote is rather evenly divided and determined largely by nonracial issues. An estimated 70 percent of the Negro vote went to Kennedy, and his Republican opponent Nixon was of the opinion that he could have won with only 5 percent more of the Negro vote (Vander Zanden *a*, p. 9). The Negro vote was decisive in several key states. Kennedy could not have carried Illinois, New Jersey, Michigan, South Carolina, or Delaware if he had received only the portion of Negro votes that had gone to Stevenson, the Democratic candidate in 1956, and loss of all these states would have cost Kennedy the election.

Legislative redistricting has taken place or will probably occur in most states as a result of the 1962 Supreme Court decision in *Baker v. Carr,* which made cases concerning state legislative districting subject to review by federal courts. Urban populations will have more nearly proportionate representation. The continued controversy on redistricting is a manifestation of deep-seated national tensions that are not unrelated to racial issues. Since Negroes outside the South are almost entirely urban, their voting strength will be increased. Negro political power in the South also is enhanced by reapportionment, because Negroes in most large cities are more politically active and can vote freely, whereas many rural and small town Negroes are still denied the franchise. The Negro gain in political power in the North is partially offset by the fact that redistricting also enhances the power of metropolitan whites who live near expanding Negro ghettos and who often oppose civil rights legislation.

The injection of racial issues into elections in the North complicates voting behavior and compromises Negro political power. To the extent that whites who live near Negro ghettos vote against candidates endorsing civil rights, the Negro vote may become an embarrassment to white politicians, especially to Democratic candidates in urban centers. These candidates must hold the votes of lower- and lower-middle-class whites with recent European or Southern backgrounds, and such voters have shown themselves to be susceptible to racist appeals. Some political observers predicted that racial concerns would shift the balance of the white vote in Northern cities in the 1964 election, but apparently other issues weighed more heavily in determining voting behavior.

The increase in the number and percentage of well-educated Negroes also has increased both aspirations and capabilities for protest and concerted action. Well-educated Negroes in the North and South remain the principal instigators of protest activity—but not of violent expressions of hostility. They are not willing to defer to uneducated whites and are generally more dissatisfied with low income and low occupational status than undereducated Negroes. Education creates tastes for travel, reading material, entertainment, better housing, and better clothing. Well-educated Negroes compare their own condition with that of their white counterparts, and the economic gap between Negroes and whites is generally greater at higher than it is at lower educational levels. Consequently, the better-educated Negroes tend to feel more deprived.

As well-educated Negroes become more numerous and have more contacts with others who are well educated, both white and Negro, aspirations and discontent are reinforced and spread to other Negroes. In many communities, there are enough educated Negroes to effect concerted action and to provide trained leadership. Because the educated reinforce one another and influence others in the community, the increase in protest activity engendered by education is greater than the increase in education.

The increase in the number and proportion of Negroes in upper-level occupations has had a similar effect. The economic gap between Negroes and whites in most upper-level occupations is greater than the gap between unskilled or semi-skilled Negroes and whites. Therefore high-status Negroes probably feel more deprived. Negro white-collar workers develop middle-class tastes and aspirations and resent deferring to and being considered inferior to blue-collar whites.

Although the failure of Negro income to rise faster and the failure of the Negro-white income gap to close appreciably are major causes of discontent, increased Negro income has augmented discontent and prompted greater protest. For instance, the increase in Negro buying power has engendered resentment of segregation and discrimination in public accommodations. So long as few Negroes could afford to patronize such places, exclusion caused little concern. By the late 1950s, however, thousands of Negroes could afford the services offered by resorts, nightclubs, restaurants, and the like, and were demanding the right to buy what they could pay for. In addition to giving incentive to protest activity, increased Negro prosperity provided greater financial support for protest. This prosperity not only increased activity, it also made the protest movement less dependent upon white support, and it removed some white-imposed restraints on particular techniques of protest. When such organizations as the NAACP and the National Urban League were financed almost entirely by white philanthropy, they could not take action that might alienate their benefactors or threaten their interests. This constraint upon Negro action has not been removed completely, because all Negro action and uplift organizations—including CORE, SCLC, and SNCC—are still somewhat dependent upon white support. However, there are enough Negroes and whites who give unqualified support so that the organizations could, if necessary, do without some white backers. For instance, the National Urban League receives much of its financial backing from white-owned corporations and local white businessmen, and critics have accused it of being incapacitated by these supporters.

Recently, however, the League has sanctioned direct action, demanded preferential hiring of Negroes, and advocated action not endorsed by the white business community. This new boldness has at least two origins: (1) the leadership of the League knows that businessmen will continue to make contributions in order to attract Negro customers and to reduce welfare costs resulting from Negro poverty, and because they would rather support the League than the more "radical" organizations; and (2) the League can now get greater support from nonbusiness sources.

In short, well-educated, prosperous, white-collar Negroes are generally more resentful of segregation and discrimination, and they are better equipped to do something about them. As the struggle for survival and satisfaction of physical needs requires less attention, time, and energy, middle-class Negroes become more aware of status needs frustrated by petty discrimination, and they can devote more resources to satisfying these needs. Their views spread to lower-status Negroes in whom new ambitions are kindled and feelings of deprivation sharpened.

One might expect the widening gap between high- and low-status Negroes to be disruptive and thereby hamper effective concerted action for racial objectives. The interests and prospects of the two groups are in many respects divergent: for the well-educated and well-qualified the future looks good, but for the uneducated and unskilled it is dismal. Furthermore, between the two classes of Negroes, there is a widening gap in values, tastes, and culture in general. But despite these seemingly countervailing facts, devotion to and agreement upon race objectives have grown among Negroes, with the exception of a few dissidents, among them the Black Muslims and the remaining "Uncle Toms."

Why has this greater unity come about? Why do Negroes of such varying circumstances identify with one another and work together for a common cause? Should not those at the top of the Negro social pyramid be expected to derive satisfaction from their position so far above other Negroes? Why do they not work only for their own advancement and ignore the problems of lower-class Negroes?

Indeed, some Negroes in privileged positions do not join wholeheartedly in the collective effort for advancement, and the efforts of middle-class Negroes are for the most part directed primarily toward changes that will benefit themselves. A few successful businessmen and professionals who serve only Negroes, who live in the ghetto, and who have only limited contacts with whites, are jealous of their position at the apex of Negro society. They feel ambivalent about being overtaken by other Negroes. The people whose deference and favor they value—in sociological terminology, their "significant others"—are mostly Negroes, and they are satisfied with their high status in the Negro community. A few other Negroes ignore the collective cause because they are accepted by prominent whites, and they do not wish to risk losing a personal advantage. E. Franklin Frazier, the late Negro sociologist, in a book first published in French in 1956, condemned the Negro middle class for forsaking the masses, for making the most of their high status in Negro society to compensate for rejection by whites (Frazier *a*, especially chap. 10).

There was truth in Frazier's description of the "black bourgeoisie," but it was exaggerated and overgeneralized. In the few years since he wrote, there has been a discernible shift toward increased identification of middle-class Negroes with the masses. Negroes who have more than average contact with whites and who have gained some acceptance in white circles apparently are the most prone to work for improvement of the race as a whole. Idealistic motives are supported by the highly educated whites who welcome them as associates. They also know that their personal status in interracial circles depends in part upon the status and reputation of the race. What they would lose in relative standing in Negro society from upward movement of lower-class Negroes, they would gain in status among whites. In any case, they cannot lose their identification with other Negroes. Rarely can they move away from predominantly Negro neighborhoods or send their children to predominantly white schools. Whether they like it or not, their fate is inextricably linked to that of other Negroes, and they can attain their personal aspirations only as the entire race advances. Ironically, the remaining discrimination against these high-status Negroes who seek acceptance in white society is in the short run beneficial to lower-class Negroes, because it sustains the alliance of high- and low-status Negroes. However, the disappearance of stigma from the Negro identity, which would be necessary for full acceptance of high-status Negroes by whites, would lower barriers to the advancement of all Negroes and in the long run would benefit all of them.

An increase in Negro contacts with whites on the job, in school, in college, and in the Armed Services—contacts not of the traditional subordinate-superordinate type—have made Negroes more sensitive to white opinion, as we have indicated, and more concerned about the reputation of the race as a whole. At the same time, these contacts have increased the tendency of Negroes to judge their condition in relation to whites rather than to other Negroes, and discontent and aspirations have grown. The movement of greater numbers of Negroes into intermediate-level jobs in the integrated economy during and following World War II increased restiveness and ambitiousness of Negroes, if only because it changed their perspective and the standards by which they judged themselves, their condition, and their way of life.

Military experience during and since World War II has been a major factor behind the changed Negro stance. During World War II many Southern Negroes served outside the South in the United States and in Europe; their experiences awakened them to the possibility of egalitarian relations. Many acquired sophistication, skills, and work experience that gave them a new orientation to civilian life. They returned from the service eager to apply their new skills in civilian jobs, and they felt frustrated if, as was often the case, they were unable to do so. After military units were integrated, military experience became an even greater influence in reorienting Negroes to the white population and in remaking their self-images. The Armed Services remain an important avenue of upward mobility, often providing educational and vocational training not otherwise available. However, rising standards of recruitment now exclude the Negroes who would benefit most from military experience and training.

As Negroes have acquired more nearly the same aspirations, goals, tastes, and standards as other Americans—in other words, as they have been assimilated into the mainstream of American culture—they have become more impatient with second-class citizenship. Their assimilation, in turn, has resulted from more and improved education, greater contacts with whites, and greater exposure to the mass media of communication.

The mass media may be more important in prompting the Negro "revolt" than is generally recognized. Almost all Negroes go to movies and most families own a television set. The media portray styles of life and consumption not directly experienced by most Negroes, and this exposure creates desires for unavailable goods and services. It gives a close-up, although not necessarily a realistic, view of life in white America, with which their own life-style does not compare favorably. Newspapers and magazines have a similar effect. In addition, they report on race issues, court rulings, pronouncements by national Negro leaders, and race incidents. Such publicity focuses the Negro's attention on his underprivileged status and makes him more resentful. The publicity given the civil rights movement by the mass media undoubtedly has increased restiveness and boldness, has disseminated new techniques of protest, and has contributed to the development of race pride and solidarity.

Some Negro intellectuals attribute the increased urgency of the drive for equality partly to the emergence of the independent Negro states in Africa. Negro Americans are more prosperous, better educated, and, in their living standards, better off in almost all respects than Negroes in the African states, and the number of Americans who have emigrated to the new states is negligible. Few Negro Americans would trade places with Africans, but many envy the Africans' autonomy and freedom from direct subordination to whites. According to C. Eric Lincoln:

> Many Negroes for whom Africa seemed as remote as the planet Jupiter now find themselves exhilarated and encouraged by the emergence of black national states in the once "dark" continent. But they also find themselves strangely threatened, for the African may leave his American brother behind as the only remaining symbol of racial inferiority, of the socially and politically *déclassé* "Black Man," left in the world. (pp. 9–10)

Negro novelist James Baldwin compared the rates of change in Africa and in the United States and concluded that "all of Africa will be free before we can get a lousy cup of coffee." (Lomax, p. 88) However, the emergence of the free African states probably affected the Negro intelligentsia (who were instrumental in the civil rights movement, to be sure) more than it did the great majority of Negroes, who were little concerned with international affairs.

All these influences have raised Negro aspirations and engendered a more urgent desire for equality. Advancement on one front has only generated impatience at lags on other fronts. What the Negro wants and feels is attainable has increased more rapidly than what he has.

An increased disparity between aspirations and attainments and a feeling that the gap could be closed got the Negro protest movement underway, and once the movement gained momentum, it became self-sustaining. Participants became imbued with an almost religious zeal, and the satisfactions of participation—a feeling of being an instrument of destiny, of working for a cause, of changing the future in association with one's fellows—became sufficient motives. The mass media spread the spirit of revolution and Negro determination and unity. Millions of Negroes watched, on television, the massive march of demonstrators to the Lincoln Memorial in August 1963. They heard Martin Luther King's stirring "I've got a dream" speech from the steps of the Memorial and were captured by the spirit of the movement.

Even the least privileged Negroes have caught the spirit of protest, but, as we have pointed out, their discontent is not tempered with optimism. Their aspirations, too, have been raised by the mass media and by observing the advancement of better educated Negroes. However, the lowest classes have attained no appreciable fulfillment of their ambitions. Beset by unemployment, or at best rewarded with stagnant or slowly rising wages, these Negroes are merely observers of an affluent society.

The civil rights movement has not affected them as it has others, even though many have in one way or another been drawn into it. The movement has tended to give them pride, enhanced self-esteem, and a temporary psychological lift, but they have gained few tangible benefits and can realistically expect few in the near future. Their problems are largely economic, and they grow out of ignorance, lack of skills, family disorganizaton, illegitimacy, poor health, overindulgence in alcohol, narcotic addiction, and other conditions that cannot be much improved by concessions won through social protest. These conditions are in large measure self-perpetuating. Employment discrimination, housing discrimination, and exploitation by landlords, merchants, loan sharks, and racketeers compound and aggravate the economic problems of lower-class Negroes, but if all discrimination and exploitation were to end, their problems would be far from solved. Neither direct action, antidiscrimination legislation, nor court rulings can help them much in the immediate future, even though these measures may bring long-range benefits to younger and future generations.

Underprivileged Negroes in the Northern ghettos have gained least from the civil rights movement. For them, the movement leads to defining all problems in racial terms, to often unconcealed hatred of whites, to rejection of more responsible and moderate Negro leaders, to susceptibility to the appeals of demagogues, and to an inclination toward violence. Such underprivileged adult Negroes and poorly supervised and unemployed young Negroes were mainly responsible for the rioting in Northern cities in the summer of 1964. Their growing hostility, now more sharply focused upon the "whitey,"* and especially upon white policemen, is expressed violently when there is an excuse, such as a real or imagined instance of police brutality. Once rioting breaks out, even normally restrained individuals may become excited and give vent to pent-up hostility. A Negro woman drawn into the Harlem rioting in July of 1964 gave the following explanation:

> I clean the white man's dirt all the time. I work for four families and some I don't care for and some I like. And Saturday I worked for some I like. And when I got home and later when the trouble began, something happened to me. I went on the roof to see what was going on. I don't know what it was, but hearing the guns I felt like something was crawling in me, like the whole damn world was no good, and the little kids and the big ones and all of us was going to get killed because we don't know what to do. And I see the cops are white and I was crying. Dear God, I am crying! And I took this pop bottle and it was empty and I threw it down on the cops, and I was crying and laughing. (*Time Magazine,* July 31, 1964, p. 11)

Communists, black nationalists, and other agitators have taken advantage of rioting, but so far, and so far as is known, they have rarely been prime movers behind outbreaks of violence.

Some increase in violence is an unavoidable byproduct of the civil rights movement as it probably would-be of any profound social change. The riots in the summer of 1964 must be viewed, therefore, in perspective of the scale of the social movement. Several lives were lost and there was much property damage, but the losses were not great compared

---

* An epithet derived from Black Muslim talk of "the blue-eyed white devil."

with the riots in Detroit and Harlem in 1943, in Chicago in 1919, and other earlier racial disturbances. The national race riot fatalities for 1964 did not approach the 38 killed in the Chicago riots of 1919. The poorest Negroes have been surprisingly tranquil in view of the disparity between their new aspirations and their immediate prospects.

The Future

During the last few decades, predictions about the Negro American generally reflected the American faith in progress and forecast continued and accelerating favorable changes. The prognosticators told the Negro that his lot would in time be better. Recently, however, some students of American race relations have questioned the inevitability of unbroken advancement. Although they do not deny that since emancipation there has been long-range improvement, both absolutely and relative to whites, they point out that the road to equality has been marked by extended static intervals and periods of deterioration. For instance, from about 1880 to 1915 Jim Crow laws spread through the South and Southern Negroes lost the franchise. During the depression of the 1930s, the economic condition of the Negro deteriorated, and during the late 1950s the economic status of Negroes relative to whites declined. Several scholars believe that there will be similar periods of reversal in the future. Some have predicted that the economic and occupational gap between Negroes and whites will widen over the next two or three decades. For instance:

If we correlate, roughly, the school dropout rate with the skill requirements of the future labor force, then we can say . . . that 30 years hence, class society in the U.S. will be predominantly color society. (Bell)

There is no clear-cut evidence that the Negro is moving inexorably toward a position of equality in the American economy; there are signs that he may·be slipping back slowly. Unless future generations of Negro youth are enabled, and motivated, to acquire the skills demanded by an industrial society, the Negro may slip back even more rapidly in the future. . . . (Killian and Grigg *b*, pp. 119–120)

There is basis for such pessimism. Mechanization and automation in industry and consequent decreased demand for unskilled and semiskilled workers are tending to push Negroes farther down in the economic hierarchy, and prospects do not seem good for an offsetting increase in Negro education and skills during the next few years. At best, a majority of adult Negroes will be rather poorly educated for another four or five decades, and in the absence of an extensive and unprecedented job retraining program, they are going to fall farther behind other Americans in economic standing.

However, as the destinies of different classes of Negroes become more diverse, it is not realistic to make predictions for the population as a whole. The future is not bright for a large percentage, perhaps a majority, of Negroes, but the well-educated and well-qualified can anticipate rapid advancement. The demand for technical and professional personnel will probably continue to exceed the supply for some time; there is enough room at the top for qualified persons of all races, and white resistance to Negro entry into top-level occupations will probably continue to be negligible. In fact, Negroes may have a slight advantage because of their display value to the employer—corporation, university, or government agency—which can claim that it does not discriminate.

However, occupational and economic advancement alone will not satisfy highly capable Negroes. They still cannot usually live where they wish and consequently cannot send their children to preferred public schools. An increase in middle-class apartment buildings in Negro neighborhoods and growth of Negro suburban developments around some cities are easing the housing problems of Negroes with annual incomes of around $8,000 or more. But middle-class families with lower incomes find it difficult to escape from the slums, and higher-income Negroes are usually excluded from choice residential areas. White resistance will not easily be overcome, even with the help of executive orders and open-occupancy legislation. Another decade may see virtual solution of the housing problems of middle-class Negroes, but demands for open occupancy are encountering resistance from some banks and other lending agencies, real estate dealers, and property owners. Despite evidence that property values in the long run do not decline when an area is opened to Negro residence (Laurenti, p. 47), the myth of damage to financial interests is tenaciously held, and the prospect of having Negro neighbors is strongly resisted.

Petty discrimination and the Jim Crow practices that middle-class Negroes find galling should soon be virtually gone except in isolated Black Belt areas of the South. Southerners are not giving up these practices without a struggle, but under pressure they are giving them up. Customary discrimination has lost the undergirding of the law, fewer Negroes are prepared to conduct themselves in a posture of absolute subordination, and the increased educational status of Negroes and whites challenges Jim Crow who cannot read or write or count.

Promising as is the future for well qualified Negroes in some ways, they may not find full social acceptance for many years, and their acceptance will be retarded by continued poverty, family disorganization, and high crime rates in the Negro lower class. Furthermore, continued interracial conflict will place strains on race relations. Well-educated Negroes have little basis for communication with the poorly educated Negro masses except in the common cause of racial concerns, and even there the common interest is in very general terms rather than in detail. Not at ease with the Negro majority, not fully accepted by whites, for some time they will have a relatively lonely and marginal existence. However, their lack of full acceptance by whites may prevent their complete estrangement from the Negro masses and may spur them to continue to work for the benefit of all Negroes.

Movement of Negroes into the highly qualified elite is becoming somewhat easier but is not so rapid that this class will soon include a large proportion of Negroes. Stubborn obstacles remain to the acquisition of skills and a good education by Negroes who grow up in the rural South and in urban slums in both the North and the South. Although token desegregation of schools may spread to almost all Southern communities, the effects upon the quality of Negro education may be, in the balance, adverse; superior pupils are likely to be drawn into predominantly white schools, which will deprive the majority of Negro pupils of stimulating contacts and competition. *De facto* segregation is likely to remain the rule in all regions and will perpetuate the lower-class Negro subculture. In addition, unless drastic remedial measures are taken, poverty, disillusionment, early child-bearing, poor home environments, and similar conditions will keep the Negro school drop-out rate far above the white rate.

Even if all discrimination were to end, the low status of poorly qualified Negroes would be self-perpetuating. Poverty, high fertility, high rates of illegitimacy, widespread family disorganization, and similar conditions that hold lower-class Negroes down could continue for decades after the influences originally responsible for them were virtually eliminated. Remedial action, such as nursery schools for slum children and distribution of contraceptive information and supplies to poor women, married and single, might help to break the vicious circle. But powerful elements in the society are opposed on principle or on the basis of cost to such remedies, and it is less than certain that bold and effective measures will be taken.

The attitudes and actions of many whites toward Negroes are likely to continue to become more favorable, partly because their economic incentives for discrimination are diminishing. Increased demand for workers at high and intermediate skill levels is keeping down competition between Negroes and whites for many kinds of jobs, and there is increasing awareness among informed whites that such products of discrimination as Negro unemployment and crime entail economic and social costs for the entire society. However, many other whites—mostly at lower skill levels—will continue to feel threatened by Negro advancement and will resist welfare measures even when they are designed to aid the poor, irrespective of race. Certain Negro demands, such as that for open occupancy, may meet increased resistance from almost all classes of whites.

There is not likely to be much slackening of the civil rights movement in the near future; any increase in white resistance will probably only increase Negro determination. However, a point of diminishing returns for civil rights activities may already have been reached in the North and West. Except in a few areas of the Deep South, the more overt and flagrant forms of discrimination that are amenable to litigation, legislation, and direct action will soon be largely removed—unless the so-called "white backlash" becomes much stronger. The remaining obstacles to Negro advancement will be more refractory than those that will have been eliminated, and the almost daily change that may be perceived in certain Border and Southern areas will no longer be possible. Then there may be a decline in the optimism of Southern Negroes and in their confidence in their leadership.* The most constructive concentration of Negro efforts at this time would be upon self-improvement and upon gaining government support for far-reaching programs of uplift. However, the Negro leadership may have difficulty in redirecting Negro efforts. Demonstrations are more exciting than efforts to eliminate the by-products of discrimination, and uplift activities provide no outlet for hostility. Negroes mobilized in a struggle against whites and who have not yet attained their goals will not

---

* A survey conducted a decade ago showed that Negroes in the South were more optimistic than those in the North (Pettigrew *b*, p. 185). This difference probably persists. There is more room for improvement in the South, and recent change has been more rapid there, especially in Texas, Florida, Tennessee, North Carolina, and other areas outside the Deep South. In many localities in the North, change has already reached the point at which it is hardly perceptible.

readily turn their efforts to conditions within the Negro population. A major challenge to the Negro leadership will be to prevent an increase in violence and in other expressive activity that hurts the Negro cause.

The interests of Negroes and of some whites will remain opposed, and some Negro gains will cause white loss of self-esteem. Negro advancement will continue to be accompanied by some interracial conflict—a fact that causes consternation among liberal whites, who seek both Negro advancement and greater harmony. Negro leaders generally realize that accelerated Negro gains and increased interracial harmony are, for the near future, incompatible goals, and they have cast their votes for Negro gains. It is not yet clear whether they will temper immediate demands for long-term objectives. The debate about conducting demonstrations during the Presidential campaign of 1964 is an example of such a strategy question.

Self-interest and, to an extent, humanitarian and ideological considerations will motivate some whites to crusade actively for Negro rights. Egalitarian values will prompt many more whites to limited support of Negro advancement that does not threaten their own interests. The underlying forces in the drama of American race relations will continue to be a complex of conflicting interests and conflicting values.

A Perspective from 1967

Recent developments have borne out the accuracy of the preceding paragraphs, which were written in 1964. The direct-action techniques of 1963–1964 probably accomplished as much as they could. As we have pointed out, there is a critical difference between circumstances that can be altered by direct action and hard-core problems. The remaining obstacles to Negro advancement are largely of the latter kind, stubborn and deeply rooted. They are embedded in the institutionalized blunders of the past. Progress in education, occupation, and the economic sphere has been continuous but slow, and its impact has been uneven, hardly reaching the most under-privileged. But even those whose lives are least affected have been caught up in the ferment of the times. Inexpressible despair has been replaced by expressed resentment. Fleeting glimmers of hope and gratitude have been followed by dis-illusionment and hostility. An initially ambitious federal war on poverty has failed to meet expectations. However, present expectations and felt needs would exceed a far more am-bitious program. The hungers of centuries are not readily satiated.

Perhaps the most important development of the last three years has been a remarkable increase in race pride and solidarity. To many whites, startled by the slogan of Black Power and disturbed by the displacement of whites from key positions in Negro action organizations, this solidarity ap-pears to be racism in reverse. White students of race relations are sometimes thrown off guard by increased sensitivity that inhibits candid discussion. Social scientists who discuss the way family disorganization impedes Negro progress or who discuss Negro-white differences in achievement are accused of scientific racism, no matter how carefully prejudice and dis-crimination are linked to the "shortcomings" of Negroes.

Another manifestation of sensitivity and solidarity is the tendency to close ranks around Negroes who incur public re-sentment. To evoke the displeasure of whites is to challenge white power, and the end justifies the means. Organizational schisms and competition between Negroes are forgotten in the face of a white "threat," whether it be by policeman, scholar, or the Congress. Increasingly Negroes present a solid front in their relations with whites. The old double standard that held Negroes guilty whenever there was conflict with whites has been turned around: conflict with whites is self-justifying. Questionable acts by Negroes in the public eye gain the sanc-tion of the civil rights movement even though the acts are irrelevant to the movement.

Coinciding with growing racial solidarity is lessened em-phasis on integration. It is unlikely that most Negroes will accept the latest doctrine of black nationalism: that middle-class American society is so corrupt and decadent that integration is an unworthy objective. However, for many spokesmen integration is not the salient goal it was in the 1950s and early 1960s, partly because it has turned out for the present to be unattainable.

Irritating though these developments may be to liberal whites who yearn for interracial harmony, they may contribute to Negro welfare if they are channeled into task-related action. Increased voting, political activity, and the election of more Negro officials are examples of such action because they foster Negro influence within the decision-making institutions of the society. Such changes enhance the capacity of Negroes to initiate and consolidate achievements and to prevent drift and the leaching away of earlier gains. With more Negroes in public office one may expect pressure for an immediate compensatory increase in the Negroes' share of rewards and resources.

The new stance of Negroes has hazardous components. Long experience as objects of violence has trained Negroes to regard violence as legitimate, and persistent white extremism invites counteraction and reprisal. The low educational status of many Negroes makes them susceptible to demagogues while the declining authority of clergymen undermines non-violent sentiment. The prediction of riot by concerned civil rights leaders blurs into threats of riot by provocators. It seems too much to hope that such an unstable mixture will fail to detonate into repeated violence and destructiveness. Then determination, humanity, and ability to adhere to long-run objectives will have their most severe test. White demands for punitive action and reprisal may jeopardize programs whose certain benefits are years or decades in the future. But perhaps the most difficult task is to sustain a sense of urgency and urgently to pursue long-range goals without the goad of violence. The resources, tenacity, and wisdom that are required to carry out the most important agenda in domestic American affairs can not be exaggerated. Expecting too much from spasmodic and impetuous efforts, piecemeal actions, and sloganeering will prolong the trial and defer the achievement.

Final verification of the transformation of the Negro American will be expressed in the absolute and relative improvement in his status and increased interaction with whites, unthreatened and unthreatening interaction between equals. These ends will be achieved at great cost, a far greater cost than has yet been offered, and they lie at a greater distance than most have been willing to admit.

Bibliography

ALEXIS, MARCUS. "Some Negro-White Differences in Consumption," *American Journal of Economics and Sociology,* 21 (January, 1962), pp. 11–28.

ALLPORT, GORDON W. *The Nature of Prejudice.* Cambridge, Mass.: Addison-Wesley, 1954.

ASHMORE, HARRY S. *The Negro and the Schools.* Chapel Hill: University of North Carolina Press, 1954.

BELL, DANIEL. "The Post-Industrial Society." Background paper, Liberty Mutual Forum on the Impact of Technological and Social Change, Boston, Massachusetts, June 14, 1962; quoted in Killian and Grigg, *b.* (see citation below).

BERRY, BREWTON. *Race and Ethnic Relations.* Boston: Houghton Mifflin, 1958.

BINDMAN, AARON M., *a.* Personal communication.

BINDMAN, AARON M., *b.* "A Study of the Negro Community in Champaign-Urbana, Illinois." Unpublished M.A. thesis, University of Illinois, 1961.

BOGUE, DONALD J. *The Population of the United States.* New York: Free Press of Glencoe, 1959.

BRAZZIEL, WILLIAM F. "Correlates of Southern Negro Personality," *Journal of Social Issues,* 20 (April, 1964), pp. 46–53.

BREARLEY, H. C. *Homicide in the United States.* Chapel Hill: University of North Carolina Press, 1932.

BRINK, WILLIAM, and LOUIS HARRIS. *The Negro Revolution in America.* New York: Simon and Schuster, 1964.

195

BROOM, LEONARD, and NORVAL D. GLENN. "Negro-White Difference in Reported Attitudes and Behavior," *Sociology and Social Research,* 50 (January, 1966), pp. 187–200.

BROOM, LEONARD, and PHILIP SELZNICK. *Sociology,* 3rd ed. New York: Harper & Row, 1963.

BURGESS, M. ELAINE, and DANIEL O. PRICE. *An American Dependency Challenge.* Chicago: American Public Welfare Association, 1963.

CAPLOVITZ, DAVID. *The Poor Pay More: Consumer Practices of Low Income Families.* New York: Free Press of Glencoe, 1963.

CAYTON, HORACE R., and GEORGE S. MITCHELL. *Black Workers and the New Unions.* Chapel Hill: University of North Carolina Press. 1939.

CLARK, JOHN P. Personal communication.

CLARK, JOHN P., and EUGENE P. WENNINGER, *a.* "Goal Orientations and Illegal Behavior Among Juveniles," *Social Forces,* 42 (October, 1963), pp. 49–59.

CLARK, JOHN P., and EUGENE P. WENNINGER, *b.* "Socio-Economic Class and Area as Correlates of Illegal Behavior Among Juveniles," *American Sociological Review,* 27 (December, 1962), pp. 826–834.

CLARK, KENNETH B. *Dark Ghetto: An Analysis of the Dilemma of Social Power.* New York: Harper & Row, 1965.

CUTHBERT, MARIAN VERA. *Education and Marginality: A Study of the Negro College Graduate.* New York: Columbia University Press, 1942.

DAVIE, MAURICE. *Negroes in American Society.* New York: McGraw-Hill, 1949.

DAVIS, ALLISON, and ROBERT J. HAVIGHURST. "Social Class and Color Differences in Childrearing," *American Sociological Review,* 11 (December, 1946), pp. 698–710.

DODDY, HURLEY H., "The Progress of the Negro in Higher Education," *Journal of Negro Education,* 32 (Fall, 1963), pp. 485–492.

DOLLARD, JOHN. *Caste and Class in a Southern Town,* 3rd ed. New York: Doubleday-Anchor, 1957.

DOYLE, BERTRAM WILBUR. *The Etiquette of Race Relations in the South: A Study in Social Control.* Chicago: University of Chicago Press, 1937.

DRAKE, ST. CLAIR, and HORACE R. CAYTON. *Black Metropolis: A Study of Negro Life in a Northern City.* New York: Harcourt, Brace & World, 1945.

EDWARDS, G. FRANKLIN. *The Negro Professional Class.* New York: Free Press of Glencoe, 1959.

ESSIEN-UDOM, E. U. *Black Nationalism: A Search for Identity in America.* Chicago: University of Chicago Press, 1962.

FRANKLIN, JOHN HOPE. *From Slavery to Freedom.* New York: Alfred A. Knopf, 1948.

FRAZIER, E. FRANKLIN, *a. Black Bourgeoisie: The Rise of a New Middle-Class in the United States.* New York: Free Press of Glencoe, 1957.

FRAZIER, E. FRANKLIN, *b. The Negro in the United States,* rev. ed. New York: Macmillan, 1957.

GALLAGHER, BUELL G., *American Caste and the Negro College.* New York: Columbia University Press, 1938.

GINZBERG, ELI, with the assistance of JAMES K. ANDERSON, DOUGLAS W. BRAY, and ROBERT W. SMUTS. *The Negro Potential.* New York: Columbia University Press, 1956.

GLENN, NORVAL D., *a.* "Negro Prestige Criteria: A Case Study in the Bases of Prestige," *American Journal of Sociology,* 68 (May, 1963), pp. 645–657.

GLENN, NORVAL D., *b.* "Negro Religion and Negro Status in the United States," in Louis Schneider, ed., *Religion, Culture, and Society.* New York: John Wiley, 1964.

GLENN, NORVAL D., *c.* "Occupational Benefits to Whites from the Subordination of Negroes," *American Sociological Review,* 28 (June, 1963), pp. 443–448.

GLENN, NORVAL D., *d.* "Some Changes in the Relative Status of American Nonwhites, 1940 to 1960," *Phylon,* 24 (Summer, 1963), pp. 109–122.

GLENN, NORVAL D., *e.* "The Relative Size of the Negro Population and Negro Occupational Status," *Social Forces,* 43 (October, 1964), pp. 42–49.

GREEN, GORDON C. "Negro Dialect, the Last Barrier to Integration," *Journal of Negro Education,* 32 (Winter, 1963), pp. 81–83.

GREENBERG, JACK. *Race Relations and American Law.* New York: Columbia University Press, 1959.

GREER, SCOTT. *Last Man In: Racial Access to Union Power.* New York: Free Press of Glencoe, 1959.

GURALNICK, LILLIAN. "The Study of Mortality by Occupation in the United States," Washington, D.C.: National Office of Vital Statistics, September, 1959.

HANDLIN, OSCAR. *Race and Nationality in American Life.* Boston: Little, Brown, 1950.

HEER, DAVID M. "The Sentiment of White Supremacy: An Ecological Study," *American Journal of Sociology,* 64 (May, 1959), pp. 592–598.

HERSKOVITS, M. J. *The Myth of the Negro Past.* New York: Harper & Row, 1941.

HOPE, JOHN, II, and EDWARD E. SHELTON. "The Negro in the Federal Government," *Journal of Negro Education,* 32 (Fall, 1963), pp. 367–374.

HUGHES, EVERETT C. "Race Relations and the Sociological Imagination," *American Sociological Review,* 28 (December, 1963), pp. 879–890.

JOHNSON, CHARLES S. *The Negro College Graduate.* Chapel Hill: University of North Carolina Press, 1938.

KILLIAN, LEWIS, and CHARLES GRIGG, *a.* "Negro Perceptions of Organizational Effectiveness," *Social Problems,* 11 (Spring, 1964), pp. 380–388.

KILLIAN, LEWIS, and CHARLES GRIGG, *b. Racial Crisis in America: Leadership in Conflict.* Englewood Cliffs, N.J.: Prentice-Hall, 1964.

KING, MARTIN LUTHER, JR. *Stride Toward Freedom: The Montgomery Story.* New York: Ballantine Books, 1958.

KINZER, ROBERT H., and EDWARD SAGARIN. *The Negro in American Business: The Conflict Between Separation and Integration.* New York: Greenberg, 1950.

KISER, CLYDE V. "Fertility Trends and Differentials Among Nonwhites in the United States," *Milbank Memorial Fund Quarterly,* 36 (April, 1958), pp. 149–197.

KLEIN, L. R., and W. H. MOONEY. "Negro-White Savings Differentials and the Consumption Function Problem," *Econometrica,* 21 (July, 1953), pp. 435–456.

KLINEBERG, OTTO, ed. *Characteristics of the American Negro.* New York: Harper & Row, 1944.

KUPER, LEO. *Passive Resistance in South Africa.* London: Jonathan Cape, 1956.

LAURENTI, LUIGI. *Property Values and Race: Studies in Seven Cities.* Berkeley: University of California Press, 1960.

LINCOLN, C. ERIC. *The Black Muslims in America.* Boston: Beacon Press, 1961.

LIPSET, SEYMOUR MARTIN, and REINHARD BENDIX. *Social Mobility in Industrial Society.* Berkeley: University of California Press, 1959.

LOGAN, RAYFORD W. *The Negro in the United States: A Brief History.* Princeton: Van Nostrand, 1957.

LOMAX, LOUIS E. *The Negro Revolt.* New York: Signet Books, 1962.

LOTT, ALBERT J., and BERNICE E. LOTT. *Negro and White Youth: A Psychological Study in a Border-State Community.* New York: Holt, Rinehart & Winston, 1963.

MACIVER, ROBERT M. *The More Perfect Union.* New York: Macmillan, 1948.

MARDEN, CHARLES F., and GLADYS MEYER. *Minorities in American Society,* 2nd ed. New York: American Book, 1962.

MARSHALL, RAY, a. "The Negro and Organized Labor," *Journal of Negro Education,* 32 (Fall, 1963), pp. 375–389.

MARSHALL, RAY, b. *The Negro and Organized Labor.* New York: John Wiley, 1965.

MCALLISTER, WILLIAM, ed. *Ayer Directory of Newspapers and Periodicals.* Philadelphia: N. W. Ayer, 1963.

MCLEAN, FRANKLIN C. Introduction to Dietrich C. Reitzes, *Negroes and Medicine.* Cambridge: Harvard University Press, 1958.

MEIER, AUGUST. "The Emergence of Negro Nationalism: A Study in Ideologies," *Midwest Journal,* 4, part I (Winter, 1951–52), pp. 96–104; part II (Summer, 1952), pp. 95–111.

MENDELSON, WALLACE. *Discrimination.* Englewood Cliffs, N.J.: Prentice-Hall, 1962.

MYRDAL, GUNNAR, with the assistance of RICHARD STERNER and ARNOLD ROSE. *An American Dilemma: The Negro Problem and Modern Democracy.* New York: Harper & Row, 1944.

National Opinion Research Center, "Jobs and Occupations: A Popular Evaluation," *Opinion News,* 9 (September 1, 1947), pp. 3–13.

NORTHRUP, HERBERT R. *Organized Labor and the Negro.* New

York: Harper & Row, 1944.

PARSONS, TALCOTT, and KENNETH B. CLARK (Eds.). *The Negro American*. Boston: Houghton Mifflin, 1966.

PETTIGREW, ANN HALLMAN, and THOMAS F. PETTIGREW. "Race, Disease, and Desegregation: A New Look," *Phylon*, 24 (Fall, 1963), pp. 315–333.

PETTIGREW, THOMAS F., *a*. "Negro American Personality: Why Isn't More Known?" *Journal of Social Issues*, 20 (April, 1964), pp. 4–23.

PETTIGREW, THOMAS F., *b*. *A Profile of the Negro American*. Princeton: Van Nostrand, 1964.

PIERCE, J. A. *Negro Business and Business Education*. New York: Harper & Row, 1947.

RECORD, C. WILSON, *a*. *The Negro and the Communist Party*. Chapel Hill: University of North Carolina Press, 1951.

RECORD, C. WILSON, *b*. *Race and Radicalism: The NAACP and the Communist Party in Conflict*. Ithaca: Cornell University Press, 1964.

REID, IRA DE A. "The American Negro," in Joseph B. Gittler, ed., *Understanding Minority Groups*. New York: John Wiley, 1956.

REITZES, DIETRICH C. *Negroes and Medicine*. Cambridge: Harvard University Press, 1958.

REUTER, EDWARD BYRON. *The American Race Problem: A Study of the Negro*, rev. ed. New York: Thomas Y. Crowell, 1938.

ROGOFF, NATALIE. "Recent Trends in Urban Occupational Mobility," in Reinhard Bendix and Seymour Martin Lipset, eds., *Class, Status and Power: A Reader in Social Stratification*. New York: Free Press of Glencoe, 1953.

ROSE, PETER I. *They and We: Racial and Ethnic Relations in the United States*. New York: Random House, 1964.

ROSEN, BERNARD C. "Race, Ethnicity, and the Achievement Syndrome," *American Sociological Review*, 24 (February, 1959), pp. 47–60.

SCHERMERHORN, R. A. *These Our People: Minorities in American Culture*. Boston: Heath, 1949.

SHAW, RAY. "The Negro Consumer," *Wall Street Journal*, June 30, 1961.

SIMPSON, GEORGE EATON, and J. MILTON YINGER. *Racial and Cultural Minorities: An Analysis of Prejudice and Discrimination,* rev. ed. New York: Harper & Row, 1958.

SMITH, CHARLES U., and JAMES W. PROTHRO. "Ethnic Differences in Authoritarian Personality," *Social Forces,* 35 (May, 1957), pp. 334–338.

TAEUBER, KARL E., and ALMA F. TAEUBER. *Negroes in Cities.* Chicago: Aldine, 1965.

THOMPSON, DANIEL C., *a.* "Career Patterns of Teachers in Negro Colleges," *Social Forces,* 36 (March, 1958), pp. 270–276.

THOMPSON, DANIEL C., *b. The Negro Leadership Class.* Englewood Cliffs, N.J.: Prentice-Hall, 1963.

THOMPSON, EDGAR T., and EVERETT C. HUGHES. *Race: Individual and Collective Behavior.* New York: Free Press of Glencoe, 1958.

TUMIN, MELVIN M., *a. Desegregation: Resistance and Readiness.* Princeton: Princeton University Press, 1958.

TUMIN, MELVIN M., *b. Segregation and Desegregation: A Digest of Recent Research.* New York: Anti-Defamation League of B'Nai B'Rith, 1957.

VANDER ZANDEN, JAMES W., *a. American Minority Relations.* New York: Ronald Press, 1963.

VANDER ZANDEN, JAMES W., *b.* "The Non-Violent Resistance Movement Against Segregation," *American Journal of Sociology,* 68 (March, 1963), pp. 544–550.

WEAVER, ROBERT C. *Negro Labor: A National Problem.* New York: Harcourt, Brace, & World, 1946.

WILLIAMS, ROBIN M., JR., with the collaboration of JOHN P. DEAN and EDWARD A. SUCHMAN. *Strangers Next Door: Ethnic Relations in American Communities.* Englewood Cliffs, N.J.: Prentice-Hall, 1964.

WILSON, JAMES Q. *Negro Politics: The Search for Leadership.* New York: Free Press of Glencoe, 1960.

WOODWARD, C. VANN. *The Strange Career of Jim Crow.* New York: Galaxy Books, 1957.

YOSHINO, I. ROGER. "The Stereotype of the Negro and His High Priced Car," *Sociology and Social Research,* 44 (November-December, 1959), pp. 112–118.

Index

COLOPHON BOOKS ON SOCIOLOGY

Charles Abrams	THE CITY IS THE FRONTIER. CN 106
Graham B. Blaine, Jr.	YOUTH AND THE HAZARDS OF AFFLUENCE: The High School and College Years. CN 118
Daniel J. Boorstin	THE IMAGE: A Guide to Pseudo-Events in America. CN 37
Kenneth E. Boulding	THE MEANING OF THE 20TH CENTURY: The Great Transition. CN 67
Leonard Broom and Norval Glenn	THE TRANSFORMATION OF THE NEGRO AMERICAN. CN 117
Stuart Chase	THE PROPER STUDY OF MANKIND: An Inquiry into the Science of Human Relations. CN 10
Stephen Clissold	LATIN AMERICA: A Cultural Outline. CN 87
Peter F. Drucker	LANDMARKS OF TOMORROW: A Report on the New "Post-Modern" World. CN 63
S. C. Dube	INDIAN VILLAGE. CN 115
Constance McLaughlin Green	THE RISE OF URBAN AMERICA. CN 113
Joel Martin Halpern	A SERBIAN VILLAGE: Social and Cultural Change in a Yugoslav Community. CN 114
Eric Hoffer	THE ORDEAL OF CHANGE. CN 35
Joseph P. Lyford	THE AIRTIGHT CAGE: A Study of New York's West Side. CN 127
Joseph P. Lyford	THE TALK IN VANDALIA: The Life of an American Town. CN 51
Willie Morris, Ed.	THE SOUTH TODAY: One Hundred Years after Appomattox. CN 84
Snell Putney and Gail J. Putney	THE ADJUSTED AMERICAN: Normal Neuroses in the Individual and Society. CN 95
Patricia Cayo Sexton	SPANISH HARLEM: Anatomy of Poverty. CN 83
Laurence Wylie	VILLAGE IN THE VAUCLUSE, rev. ed. CN 24